CARTIER CARTEL 3

SOUTH BEACH SLAUGHTER

BUY

FOR MELODRAMA

CARTIER CARTEL 3

SOUTH BEACH SLAUGHTER

Cartier Cartel 3: South Beach Slaughter. Copyright © 2013 by Melodrama Publishing. All rights reserved. Printed in the United States of America. No part of this book may be used or reproduced in any manner whatsoever without written permission except in the case of brief quotations embodied in critical articles or reviews. For information, address Melodrama Publishing, P.O. Box 522, Bellport, NY 11713.

www.melodramapublishing.com

Library of Congress Control Number: 2013946111
ISBN-13: 978-1620780275
ISBN-10: 1620780275
First Edition: November 2013
10 9 8 7 6 5 4 3 2 1

Interior Design: Candace K. Cottrell
Cover Design: Marion Designs
Cover Model: Latecia Black

BOOKS BY NISA SANTIAGO

CHAPTER 1

Miami, Florida, with its sandy beaches, year-round warm weather, and alluring club life was a direct contrast to the cold, changeable weather of Philadelphia. Cartier had nothing against Philly, but Miami was a better town for her. Not only was she tired of the cold and snow, but Philly was also too close to New York. Wanting the best for her family, she needed to be somewhere far from New York and away from the turbulent lifestyle she'd once lived. That meant staying out of the game and keeping a low profile. The violence and the killings had taken a toll on her and her family, so she wanted to put as much distance as possible between herself and her beloved Brooklyn.

She'd only lasted a few months in Philly, until one day she came upon Shorty Dip, a familiar face from Brooklyn who recognized her. There was no telling who was still holding grudges. That spooked her. Cartier had made a lot of enemies up North, and to constantly have to look over her shoulder wasn't something she wanted for her family. Especially with young kids to care for. After Jason got himself murdered and Cartier got herself and Christian shot up, Cartier had never felt so vulnerable. Losing Monya, Shanine, Bam and finally Jason made her will to live that much stronger.

Cartier packed up her things and, along with her mother, Trina, her daughter, Christian, and her sisters Fendi and Prada, headed down I-95 until there wasn't any more highway left to travel. Janet, Trina's best friend and Monya's mother, said she couldn't bear to be so far away from her grandson, Jason Jr., so, reluctantly, Cartier agreed to have her step son in Miami six weeks out of each summer.

It was only a matter of weeks before Cartier and Trina clashed. You see, Miami is a party town and the weather is always hot and tropical. The problem was that there were two mothers: Cartier and Trina—and neither one wanted to parent.

"Now you done gone out every night this week, Cartier. Ain't nobody your live-in nanny!" Trina barked. She was heated because she wanted to hit the clubs so she could meet some of these Puerto Rican or Cuban men that were floating around the city. Trina was more than ready to get her fuck on. "You got a daughter to look after."

"And you don't? Last I checked, Fendi and Prada call you 'Mommy'!"

"Cartier, you better watch your mouth . . ."

"Look who's talking!"

"That's right, I'm talking!" Trina exploded. "I take care of mines!"

Cartier rolled her eyes. "No, I take care of you and yours, and mines! So if I want to go out every now and then to shake my ass, you should be a little more understanding."

"What the fuck you just said, bitch?"

"Which part didn't you hear?"

Cartier was being belligerent, which drove Trina bananas. "Keep it up, Cartier, and I'ma put my foot in ya ass!"

"You in here screaming and acting all dumb 'cuz I wanna go out? Why you hatin'?" Cartier took one last look in the mirror at her silhouette. "You too old to be hitting the club anyways. Ain't no niggas gonna be checking for you."

Trina's feelings were a little hurt. When she looked in the mirror, she saw a good-looking female staring back at her. She didn't think she looked like a fortysomething grandmother and mother of three. The word *old* stung. She marched into her bedroom, overlooking the Atlantic Ocean, and called her best friend.

Cartier could hear her mother get on the phone with Janet. Trina began to tell her how she was moving back to Brooklyn and how ungrateful Cartier was after all she'd done for her.

"That li'l ugly bitch think she cute," Trina could be heard saying. "I'ma leave her bad-luck ass right in this city! She think these new Puerto Rican muthafuckers like her stink-ass Brooklyn attitude? She gonna get a rude awakening!"

The gleaming black Range Rover made its way across the MacArthur Causeway, headed toward South Beach. The eighty-five-thousand-dollar truck was a gift to herself. Cartier always moved around in style, and she had enough cash to splurge on herself and her family. She was living large off the money she'd found in the safe-deposit box that belonged to her dead husband, Jason. It was enough money to keep her afloat and to continue living the diva lifestyle for a long while. She had her peoples staying in a high-rise condo on Brickell Avenue, a thirty-five-story building that offered an unobstructed view of the ever-changing Miami skyline.

Cartier was proud of her accomplishments. She was one of a select few to leave the game alive and still live a life of luxury with her family. She had paid her dues in the streets, doing her dirt, busting her gun, surviving an assassination attempt, and even serving seven years in prison. Now it was time to live happily ever after. But Cartier knew life wasn't a fairy tale, and even though Miami was miles away from Brooklyn, she had sense enough to know that danger was everywhere, so she kept her gun close at all times.

She felt like a queen in her black chariot with "Started From the Bottom" by Drake blasting in the truck. The weather was warm and balmy, and she was ready to show off the shape she got from her momma. Clad in a form-fitting dress that hugged her luscious curves, her red-bottoms pressed against the accelerator, taking the Range Rover to 75 mph.

The sun had set long ago, creating a temperate evening over the city of Miami, which had lit up in a colorful hue that could be seen from miles away. The closer Cartier drove toward South Beach, the thicker the traffic became. South Beach was a major destination for both American and international tourists, with hundreds of nightclubs, restaurants, boutiques, and hotels.

A brown-skinned cutie in her late twenties, Cartier knew she could never get tired of the club scene. She'd done the wife thing—which didn't work out. She'd tried the "hold your man down while he's locked down" thing—which didn't work out. Now, she was doing her—which seemed to be working out great. She looked good and felt terrific. Cartier knew that Trina was getting fed up, but it wasn't anything a shopping spree and some quality family time couldn't fix.

She came to a stop in front of Buck 15, a small underground bar and lounge with artistic furnishing and a loft feel. Her pricey Range Rover blended in smoothly with the Rolls-Royce Phantom, cocaine-colored Bentley, S550 Benz, Corvettes, Porsches, and Audi Q7s parked on the busy street. She stepped out of her truck feeling like a celebrity. The second her pricey red-bottoms touched the pavement, all eyes were on her. She strutted toward the front entrance with a smirk. She was so Brooklyn.

Cartier was cool with one of the security guards and eased inside. She was extra happy tonight. She was excited about her good friend, Li'l Mama, flying in tomorrow evening from New York into Miami International. It had been a long while since the two founding members from the Cartier Cartel had seen each other, so they had a lot of catching up to do.

Buck 15 was blaring with Flo Rida, and the patrons were jumping up and down, bouncing around the place, looking electrified. Cartier's eyes scanned the club, searching for Quinn, who had to be nowhere else but in the VIP section, where she lived and breathed, popping bottles with her peoples. Cartier strutted toward the VIP area, moving through the thick crowd. Bitches were hating—giving hard stares—and niggas were craving to push up. Cartier had edge that didn't go unnoticed. It was a mix of sex appeal and grit. As the strobe lights bounced off her, the crowd parted to allow her through.

She spotted her girl Quinn seated in the VIP, surrounded by the Ghost Ridas, her brother's Miami gang. Since Cartier's arrival in Miami, Quinn had become a really good friend to her. The two had met in Club 01 a few months earlier. That night Quinn had complimented Cartier on her shoes, and they started talking, and had become inseparable.

Quinn, Mexican-born and Miami-raised, was a female with a body to die for. She had raven-black hair, tanned skin, and dark, hypnotic eyes that could cut through a brick wall. At five eight, she was definitely eye candy in the club in her deep purple low-cut dress with the ultra-plunging neckline. Her strong, defined legs stretched out in a pair of Fendi pumps.

Quinn had a strong predilection for the brothers. In fact, she loved to have a big, black dick inside of her. There was something about the brothers that made her weak, which sometimes caused unrest with her blood brother and his gang. But Quinn didn't give a fuck. She had earned their respect, because she was a bad bitch who was down for whatever. She downed her umpteenth drink, laughing with the Ghost Ridas, over a dozen deep and sporting their gang colors, purple and black.

As Cartier stepped inside the area, Quinn shouted out, "Is that my fuckin' bitch right there?" She stood up to greet Cartier with a hug and kisses to both cheeks.

"Hey, Quinn," Cartier greeted with a smile.

"Have a seat, bitch," Quinn said jokingly. "What you drinking?"

Having grown up around killers all her life, Cartier took her seat among the wolves. Any friend of Quinn's was a friend of hers.

Quinn removed the Moët bottle from its icy chill and poured Cartier a glass, while the tattooed gangsters of the Ghost Ridas, clad in leather vests, purple Ts, jeans and heavy jewelry were laughing it up and drinking heavily.

Cartier leaned back against the soft-cushioned banquette that ran along the VIP room and crossed her legs. Her eyes scanned the room, looking for any dude with potential. There was so much money inside the club; so many niggas who were boss of their empires, just as Cartier was boss of hers. She took a sip of Moët, as the club came alive to Rihanna's "Diamonds."

"So, your friend from New York is comin' tomorrow, right?" Quinn asked.

Cartier nodded. "Yup."

"You need me to roll wit' you?"

"If you want."

"Bitch, you know I'm down."

Cartier was happy to hear that. She was hoping that the two didn't bump heads and would get along with each other, knowing that Li'l Mama could be rough around the edges and that Quinn was a hardcore bitch. The last thing she needed was some beef between her longtime friend and her newfound friend.

"Hey, Quinn, who's the *chola*?" one of the Ghost Ridas asked, eyeing Cartier like she was his property. "She down to get wit' the homies?"

Cartier looked up at the man unperturbed.

Quinn erupted with, "Yo, Tumble, chill ay, you my *vato*, but don't play my homegirl. You drunk, yo. Fall back." She stood up to make her point clear.

Tumble stood over six feet tall, and he was muscular, with two dark teardrops under his right eye. He was clutching a bottle of Henny Black in his hand. It was evident he was a little tipsy.

Tumble glanced at Cartier. "*Chido*. No disrespect, Quinn." He took a few steps back. "Maybe another time."

Cartier already knew his type. He was a killer. It showed in his eyes, and was literally written on his face. Though Quinn had the leash around him tight, Cartier knew he was the type of dude that didn't ask for permission to get what he wanted.

"Don't mind him, Cartier," Quinn said, moving her hands around wildly. "He a fool. Nigga knows better than to disrespect any of my peoples."

"I'm cool, Quinn." Cartier shrugged her shoulders, dismissively. "It ain't even that serious."

"I feel you, mama." A now more relaxed Quinn took a swig from the Moët bottle.

Cartier was on her third drink and feeling nice. When she felt her iPhone vibrate and ring in her clutch, she quickly reached into it to answer the call. There was no number on her caller ID, but she answered anyway, plugging one finger into her left ear and leaning over with the phone against her right.

"Hello," she said, trying to hear over the earsplitting music. "Hello," she repeated, but there was nothing but silence on the other end. She looked down to see the screen pop up on her phone. The caller had hung up.

Cartier tossed her phone back into her clutch, looking somewhat worried. It was the third such phone call she'd received this evening.

"You okay?" Quinn asked.

She nodded.

Cartier sat for a moment, her high spirits changing somewhat. She began to think about her family. She tapped Quinn on her shoulder. "I gotta make a phone call. I'll be in the bathroom."

"You sure everything's okay?" Quinn repeated with concern.

"Yeah. I just gotta call home."

Cartier stood up and hurried from the VIP area and walked toward the ladies' bathroom. She pushed the door open and went into her clutch again and pulled out her cell phone. She leaned against the sink and dialed home.

The phone rang three times then Trina picked up. "What, Cartier?"

"Ma, everything okay?"

"Yeah, everything's okay. Why you asking?"

"I dunno. Where's Christian?"

"I just put her ass to bed. She's fast asleep. What's wrong?"

"Nothing . . ."

"You sure?"

"Yeah."

"Ya ass feeling guilty, right? 'Cuz you keep leaving me in here to babysit these kids."

"Nah, it ain't even like that. I just had a strange feeling."

"Don't worry about us, Cartier," Trina said coolly. "This ain't New York. Nobody knows us down here. Everything's fine. Go and have a good time. I'm here watchin' a movie and the house is quiet."

"Okay, Ma. Thanks. I'll see you later."

Cartier hung up, feeling somewhat relieved, but that strange feeling still swirled around in her stomach. She turned to look at her image in the large mirror, sighing heavily. She was alone in the bathroom and could hear the muffled music from the club. She checked herself quickly and applied more lip gloss to her full lips. "I need some fuckin' dick. I'm turning into an uptight, paranoid bitch," she chuckled to herself as she walked out.

As the party continued, Cartier had a nice chat with Ranger, a well-respected O.G. in Ghost Ridas. In his mid-thirties, he was Miami-born with Mexican and Dominican blood. Swathed with gang tattoos and nice jewelry, he stood six-four.

Cartier was enjoying their talk, but then she noticed she was being watched by a dark stranger from across the bar. His gaze was intense. When she returned his stare, he never broke eye contact. At first she expected his eyes to soften; perhaps he would walk over and push up or, as a flirty gesture, send her a bottle of champagne. So it came, at first, as a blow to her ego. And then the hair on the back of her neck began to stand up. If he wanted her to be intimidated, she wasn't going to show it. He glared and she glared back.

Ranger noticed she was distracted, and then he noticed the distraction. "You know dude?"

Cartier shook her head.

Ranger took off with Cartier on his heels. She was drunk and was ready to set it off. Club or no club, she wanted it to go down.

The dark stranger, who was nursing a beer at the edge of the bar, didn't flinch. As the couple approached he stood his ground.

"Yo, homes, you got a problem wit' my lady?"

The man slowly turned to see that he was surrounded by Ranger, Cartier, and now a few Ghost Ridas. He removed himself from the barstool but kept a cool demeanor. "No," he said. "No problem with her at all. My bad if I offended anyone."

"Leave, muthafucka, before I let loose some of my goons and you won't leave at all."

The man smirked and held up his hands in surrender. "Not a problem."

Cartier wasn't going to allow it to end so easily. She picked up a random drink and tossed it into his face.

"Do we have a problem now?"

The man wiped the dripping liquid off his dark-chocolate skin and gritted his teeth.

"Nah, we still don't have a problem."

Had this been a New York nightclub, he would have had his guts stomped out. Cartier was wondering what she had to do for the Ghost Ridas to teach this lame-ass dude a lesson. She could see something in his eyes that she didn't like. Had the Cartel been at her side, he would have been shot or stabbed the fuck up by now. From her peripheral vision she could see security trying to make their way through the crowd.

Amped up on liquid courage, Cartier wanted to fan the fire. She lunged toward him but was held back by Ranger. He grabbed both her wrists as she tried to swing, wildly. Cartier looked, and Quinn wasn't anywhere to be found, which left a salty taste in her mouth. There was an unspoken code between girlfriends—have my back at all times!

"Ay, yo! Chill, mama!" Ranger said, as he struggled with the feisty female.

Cartier watched as the stranger backpedaled toward the door before he made his exit. He glanced at Cartier one last time, took his index finger and made a sweeping *slit your throat* gesture, sending a creepy chill down her spine. He had New York written all over him. She knew he could be trouble.

"Did you see what he just did?!" she screamed. "He said he's gonna kill me!"

The Ghost Ridas looked at the young troublemaker and shrugged off her theatrics. She wasn't one of them.

They came out tonight to have a good time and at the moment she was blowing everyone's high. They flexed their presence and authority and was shown respect without busting their guns or creating chaos. Truth be told, neither one of them was ready to make the papers defending a black chick from up North.

Cartier was furious. She sulked around the club until she found Quinn, hemmed up against a wall with some dude whispering in her ear.

Cartier roared, "Where the fuck you been?"

Quinn was taken aback. Surely Cartier wasn't talking to her. "Huh?"

"Yo, I'm out."

Quinn blinked a couple times. "Why you leavin', chica? You just got here."

Cartier rolled her eyes and pushed her way through the crowd. Originally, she was going to ask Quinn to gather up a few Ridas and walk her to her car. But at the moment, she was so heated and filled with so much anger and rage that she didn't want any backup. She was in *I wish a nigga would* mode.

Cartier exited the club and rushed home to check on her family. She entered the condo and found her mother sleeping on the couch and Fendi, Prada, and Christian asleep in their bedrooms.

She was somewhat relieved, but she couldn't get over the creep from the club. What was that all about? And why wasn't Quinn around to have her back? Did she not notice all the commotion in the club? For Quinn to have all of a sudden disappeared didn't sit too well with Cartier.

As Cartier peeled off her clothes and hopped into a much-needed hot shower, the only silver lining was that her one true friend, Li'l Mama, would be arriving, tomorrow. She couldn't wait for their reunion.

CHAPTER 2

Cartier navigated her truck toward the busy terminal of Miami International Airport. She couldn't stop beaming. She was moments away from seeing Li'l Mama again. It was a beautiful day, and the weather was a gentle calm, the vast blue sky covering all of Miami.

Quinn rode quietly in the passenger's seat as Alicia Keys' "Brand New Me" roared through the speakers of the truck. Cartier still wasn't feeling Quinn from last night. She kept glancing over at Quinn and her big-ass pie-face and wanted to bash her teeth in. But she chilled. Flipping on Quinn would cause all types of unwanted heat from the Ghost Ridas.

Quinn placed a wet daddy — weed soaked in formaldehyde — between her lips, lit it up, and took a few pulls. She then passed it to Cartier as she drove into the airport's parking garage.

The two ladies stepped onto the garage pavement and made their way toward the busy terminal, their eyes a bit seedy from the laced weed. Cartier couldn't enter the terminal fast enough. Quinn trailed right behind her.

The two ladies were immediately swallowed up in the south terminal by the buzz of arriving passengers and their family and friends, employees, and security personnel.

Cartier searched for Li'l Mama's flight detail on the large board. "It already landed," she said to Quinn.

"Where she at then?"

Cartier turned her attention to the hoard of passengers that poured into the terminal like a flash flood, with scattered cheers from individuals reuniting with family or friends. She focused her attention on every last passenger, trying to pick out Li'l Mama. The corners of her mouth curled up when she finally saw Li'l Mama walking behind the crowd, pulling Louis Vuitton rolling luggage while chatting on her cell phone, dressed in black leggings, a Stella McCartney halter top, and stilettos.

Their eyes met, and Cartier hurried toward Li'l Mama and embraced her longtime friend in a strong hug. "Bitch, it took you long enough to get here," Cartier cried out.

"Shit. Look who's talking . . . wit' ya paranoid ass. Took you long enough to invite a bitch down," Li'l Mama replied lightheartedly. "But I know you were only being cautious."

They continued to embrace each other like schoolgirls, talking shit. Cartier couldn't believe her eyes. It was about time. Finally, a familiar face from her old circle was there to join her in Miami.

As Quinn walked over to the joyous reunion, jealousy panged throughout her veins. Her deadpan stare gave Li'l Mama pause. She pulled herself away from Cartier and gazed at her.

"And who's this?" Li'l Mama asked dryly.

"Li'l Mama, this is Quinn." Cartier smiled. "Quinn, this is Li'l Mama."

"Hey, I've heard a lot about you," Quinn said, forcing a smile and extending her hand for a handshake.

"Really? I can't say the same thing," Li'l Mama replied matter-of-factly, leaving Quinn's hand suspended in air.

Quinn forced a halfhearted smile.

"Enough of the small talk. We got shopping to do, ballers to meet, and great food to taste," Cartier exclaimed excitedly. "In other words, we gonna run through South Beach."

The trio walked toward the exit of the terminal. Li'l Mama and Cartier did most of the talking while Quinn walked a few steps behind, suddenly feeling like the stepsister. Cartier was telling her friend all about Miami, the people, and the weather, until her cell phone rang, revealing the same blocked caller. She stopped her conversation to answer, but there was no reply. Cartier became vexed.

"You okay, Cartier?" Li'l Mama asked.

"I'm okay," Cartier replied faintly.

The trio continued walking toward the black-on-black Range Rover, Cartier's mood changing from happy to annoyed.

When they entered the parking garage, Li'l Mama said, "Damn, bitch, you got a ticket on your windshield."

Cartier sucked her teeth. "How they gonna ticket my ass and this is paid parking!"

She stared at the paper placed between her windshield and her wipers. Furious, she snatched it and started to read it. The more she read, the bigger her eyes became. "No!" she screamed out, before falling against her truck, feeling faint.

Li'l Mama and Quinn looked dumbfounded. All the theatrics over a ticket?

"Cartier, what's up, yo?" Li'l Mama shouted. "How much is it?"

"They took her," Cartier whispered.

"Huh? Took what?"

Quinn removed the note from Cartier's hand and started to read it:

GO TO THE POLICE, SHE'S DEAD. CONTACT YOUR GOONS, SHE'S DEAD. TRY COMING AFTER US AND YOU'LL BE FINDING YOUR DAUGHTER'S BODY PARTS ALL AROUND THIS CITY.

Cartier's worst fear had just come true—her daughter had been kidnapped.

CHAPTER 3

Cartier's foot was glued to the accelerator, doing 85 mph on the 395 highway. She swerved the Range Rover in and out of traffic like race car driver Danica Patrick, her cell phone against her ear. She called home over and over, but her house phone kept going to voice mail.

"No one's pickin' the fuck up!" she screamed out.

"Don't worry," Quinn exclaimed. "We gonna get there and handle this."

With tears flooding her eyes, Cartier rushed toward her home, trying not to think the worst. She tried calling home again.

"Pick up! Pick up! Pick the fuck up!" she screamed out, hearing the house phone ring and ring.

Li'l Mama slid in the backseat as the truck made hairpin turns. "Cartier, just chill out."

"Don't tell me to chill out, Li'l Mama! They got my fuckin' daughter!"

The event had all three girls clueless. Quinn wanted to call her brother, but Cartier was against it. She wanted to follow the note's instruction, but her first priority was to go home to see if the note was a hoax.

She brought the Range Rover to a screeching stop in front of the high-rise, threw the gear into park, and bolted from the truck, with Quinn and Li'l Mama right on her heels. The girls ran into the lobby and thrust themselves into the elevator.

"Please, God, please let them be okay. Please, God, let them be okay, please let them be okay," Cartier chanted with teary eyes.

Quinn and Li'l Mama were quiet, but the look on their faces spoke volumes. They had the same uneasiness as their friend.

The elevator came to a stop on the 35th floor, and before the doors were completely open, Cartier sprinted from the lift and ran toward her apartment, where she found the door ajar. She pushed the door open and rushed inside, only to witness the massacre that had occurred.

Cartier took a few steps into the apartment with its blood-spattered walls and collapsed to her knees at the sight of her slaughtered family.

"Noooo!" she screamed out. "Nooooooo. God nooooooo!"

Quinn and Li'l Mama rushed into the apartment. Their eyes widened at the bloody scene.

"Ohmygod," Li'l Mama stammered.

Cartier's apartment looked like a scene out of *Friday the 13th*—the posh cream carpet coated with blood, broken glass everywhere, overturned furniture, walls smashed in, and her two sisters, Prada and Fendi, sprawled out naked on their backs, duct tape around their wrists, their throats slit from ear to ear.

The vision of the guy in the club making the throat slit gesture came bursting back into Cartier's memory.

"He warned me . . ." Cartier said. "He fucking warned me!"

"Who warned you?" Li'l Mama wanted to know. "What are you talking about? Who did this?"

Cartier wanted to lash out at Quinn. She needed somebody to blame, but she quickly realized that she was at someone's mercy. And if Quinn was behind this carnage, she needed to cage her temper until she got the answers she needed.

Ignoring Li'l Mama's questions, she replied, "Where's Trina and Christian?"

The three separated and went room to room. They found Trina naked in the master bedroom, numerous stab wounds, bloody from head to toe, her wrists tied to the bedposts, her face bashed in almost beyond recognition. As her chest heaved up and down, blood bubbles popped out. It was a frightening sight.

Cartier screamed out for her daughter, "Christian!" running from room to room, but there wasn't any answer.

Quinn was ready to phone her brother, an ambulance, the police —somebody to help with what her brain was trying to process. Cartier snatched the phone from her hand and tossed it across the room.

"Don't call anybody!" she screamed. "The first person who picks up the phone again is getting fucked up!"

Both women remained silent, until Li'l Mama said, observantly, "They were lookin' for something."

"Lookin' for what?" Cartier shouted.

"Money, perhaps?"

"Money?" Cartier was bewildered. So many thoughts went through her mind. Was this a home invasion? Just as fast as the thought entered, it exited. Usually with a home invasion all victims were duct taped and shot execution-style. It was quick. In and out. Cartier looked around at the torture and carnage; it was too drawn out and painstaking. Couple that with the blocked phone calls and elusive stranger last night at the bar, and it wasn't adding up to the average home invasion.

"We need to do something, Cartier," Quinn exclaimed.

"I need to find my fuckin' daughter!"

Cartier knew Li'l Mama was right though. The culprits were probably looking for money, but she didn't understand who would want to do harm to her and her family in Miami. She'd assumed that all of her enemies were dead. And even so, she had taken extra precaution to maintain her family's safety by moving to a building that was supposed to have some sort of security. And the only people, outside her immediate family, who knew she had drug money was Jason and Li'l Mama. And Jason was dead. It didn't add up.

Li'l Mama said, "We gotta call somebody, Cartier. I know you don't want to, but we ain't got much choice."

Cartier didn't know what to do. Her luxurious top-floor apartment had been turned into a slaughterhouse, her family having been butchered like pigs, and her daughter was missing. She burst into tears. A heartfelt cry out of desperation. Her mother was dying in the other room, her sisters were dead, and her only child was missing.

"They said they would kill my daughter if we made any calls!"

Li'l Mama had to keep it real. "Cartier, your mother is clinging onto her life in the other room. One thing is a fact. And that is at this very moment Trina is still alive. We can't say the same thing about Christian. We have to call for help . . ."

The harsh words and realization that Li'l Mama spoke truth sent Cartier over the edge. She was stuck between being a mother to Christian and a daughter to Trina. Whose life was worth more? Quinn was trying to console her friend, but Cartier was inconsolable. With her bloodshot, tear-stained eyes, she shot a wicked look at Li'l Mama and screamed out, "Who else knew you was coming to Miami to see me? Who you tell about comin' down here, Li'l Mama?"

"What?" Li'l Mama said, dumbfounded by Cartier's remark.

Cartier rushed toward Li'l Mama in rage and grabbed her violently, shouting, "You set us up, didn't you?"

Li'l Mama pushed Cartier back. "Get the fuck off me, Cartier! What the fuck is wrong with you!"

Quinn quickly stepped in before they could tear each other's throats out.

Li'l Mama was mad. "You like a fuckin' sister to me, Cartier. You think I had a fuckin' hand in this? Are you crazy?"

Cartier knew she was right. She wasn't thinking rationally. She fell against the wall in defeat.

Quinn went up to her with concerned eyes, but before Quinn could say anything, Cartier shouted, "Stay the fuck away from me, Quinn!" Cartier's paranoia was getting the best of her. "You could be down with this shit too!"

"I'm gonna ignore that 'cuz I know shit just got crazy for you."

"Bitch, you sayin' that like you giving me a warning or some shit!" Cartier began to walk toward Quinn when her phone rang loudly. The three women stared at the purse on the floor, hearing the cell phone buzzing and ringing inside.

Cartier rushed to answer it. She snatched out the phone and hurriedly pushed the answer button. She heard somebody say, "Have we gotten your attention?"

"Where's my fucking daughter?!" she shouted.

"She's in one piece . . . for now."

The voice on the other end was distorted purposely. Quinn and Li'l Mama went to stand next to Cartier. They tried to listen in on the conversation, but it was hard to understand what was being said.

"What do you want?" Cartier asked with deep grief.

"One million in cash. You have six days to come up with it."

"I don't have—"

"Don't lie to me, bitch!"

"I don't have a million dollars in cash. I swear on my life! I have properties, investments but not that much liquid."

There was a deep, hearty laugh. "Then she will die."

Cartier cried out, "Wait! Let me talk to my daughter. Let me talk to her!"

"You have six days. Not one moment more."

"Please, let me speak with Christian. I need proof of life!"

The caller abruptly hung up.

"What did they say?" Li'l Mama asked.

Cartier was too heartbroken to reply. She felt faint. She stumbled on her feet. Li'l Mama grabbed her by the arm.

Quinn said, "Cartier, why are they doing this? Talk to us. What the fuck they told you?"

Quinn and Li'l Mama both tried to soothe Cartier, but their own tempers were flaring up. They were aching to see all those responsible for this slaughtered. How could you come in and kill two kids and their mother over money? And then kidnap a little child? They had to be monsters to do something so low. It was one thing to go after those in the drug game. That was always expected. But when you started murdering and kidnapping babies, you'd crossed the line.

The two ladies continued asking questions, but Cartier was at a loss for words. She just placed her head into her hands and began sobbing as only a mother could for her child.

CHAPTER 4

Miami-Dade police and homicide detectives flooded the lavish apartment. The gruesome scene would make even experienced officers cringe. Two suited professionals wearing latex gloves were crouched over the mutilated sisters, Prada and Fendi, inspecting the naked bodies closely.

One cop let loose a deep sigh. "Damn shame. Fuckin' city overrun with animals."

Detectives also dusted for fingerprints and snapped pictures of the bodies and the room. The coroner was bringing in body bags, but surprisingly, EMS workers were pushing a gurney into the bedroom.

"We got a pulse in here," one of the EMS workers shouted.

Miraculously, Trina was clinging to life, even with all the trauma her body had sustained.

Cartier stared hopefully at her moms, praying she'd pull through. She felt helpless and lost. Quinn and Li'l Mama refused to leave her side. She sat slumped in the living-room chair, the horror of her family's murders making her visibly sick. With her place teeming with unfamiliar faces, she wanted to wake up from her nightmare, but the crackling of a police radio and the smell of dried blood kept her in the moment.

Two detectives approached Cartier with uneasiness in their eyes. Detectives Lam and Sharp were both fifteen-year veterans on the police force, spending ten years in homicide. Each had seen his fair share of horror.

Detective Lam was a tall white man in his early forties. He had dark, deep-set eyes, and his head was bald. He also had a thick, grayish goatee. Clad in an Italian wool flannel suit, he flanked his partner Sharp and said, "Miss, our condolences, but we need to ask you a few questions."

"It won't take long," Detective Sharp chimed in.

Detective Sharp was a strikingly handsome black male detective in his mid- forties. He stood six-three with a trimmed beard and was dressed in a two-button wool blazer and a chestnut fedora. "Could we get your name, please?"

In a low, barely audible voice, she replied, "Cartier . . . Cartier Timmons."

"Okay, thank you. Do you have any idea who's responsible for this? A friend, relative? There doesn't seem to be any forced entry."

Quinn and Li'l Mama frowned at the detectives.

"Can't this fuckin' wait?" Li'l Mama barked.

Sharp replied coolly, "We want to catch these monsters, and the more information we have, the better our chances of apprehending them."

"She ain't up to talkin' right now," Quinn intervened. "Look at her."

Detective Sharp sighed heavily. "We're just trying to do our job here, ladies," he said gently.

"Well, now is not the time to do it," Li'l Mama stated. "She lost her whole fuckin' family, and y'all wanna interrogate her now? It ain't fuckin' happenin'!"

Both detectives looked at each other.

Detective Sharp knew it was never easy to get a witness or family member to cooperate after the tragic loss of a family member. He reached into his suit's inner pocket and pulled out a card. "Ladies, here's my card. You need to contact me as soon as possible. But we gonna need a statement from someone in this room."

Quinn volunteered. She went with the detectives in the next room, while Li'l Mama stayed behind to comfort Cartier, who didn't want to tell them about Christian being kidnapped. She feared that police involvement would guarantee her little girl's death. It was eating her up inside that she couldn't protect her daughter. She'd failed her. But she was determined to find her daughter, via the streets if possible.

She stood up and walked toward the floor-to-ceiling windows in the room. She then slid back the door to the balcony and stepped out onto the long, square platform. Li'l Mama followed her outside. Cartier stood erect and gazed at the multihued skyline of Miami, her eyes transfixed at the city, while damn near half of Miami-Dade was running through her home investigating the violent homicides.

"Cartier, you gonna be okay?" Li'l Mama asked.

"My daughter's out there somewhere, Li'l Mama," she said softly. "I gotta find her."

"We gonna find her. I'm here, Cartier, and you know I'll tear this muthafuckin' city apart to find Cee Cee. And whoever's responsible for this shit, hell is gonna feel like fuckin' heaven when we get done wit' them," Li'l Mama growled.

Cartier didn't respond. She was spent. She kept her sad gaze fixed on the city of Miami, thinking how vast it looked. Would she ever see Christian again? How were the kidnappers treating her? Was she afraid? Being fed? Tortured? A million uncertainties darted back and forth in her mind. She gripped the railing tightly, anger and hatred flowing through her like a shot of electricity. Once again, someone had had the audacity to come at her and destroy her family.

"Whoever's behind this shit, they are fuckin' dead," she said through clenched teeth. "They don't know who they fucked wit'!"

Li'l Mama nodded in agreement.

Quinn soon joined them on the balcony. She informed them it was time to leave. The cops had a job to do, and the trio had theirs to do also.

Little Havana was home to many Cuban immigrants, as well as many residents from Central and South America. It was also home to Quinn. She felt safe in the Latin neighborhood because her brother and the Ghost Ridas carried a strong influence among the residents and the underworld.

Quinn pulled into the narrow driveway of the brown, split-level home with the stucco rooftop in her black Yukon, which sat on 24-inch chrome rims. The windows were tinted, making it hard to see the occupants inside. It was after midnight, and the streets were pretty much barren. Quinn lived near Maximo Gomez Park, where elderly residents played high-speed dominoes, and the heady scent of the many cigars smoked there lingered like a thick fog.

Quinn, Li'l Mama, and Cartier climbed out of the truck and walked toward the front entrance. Inside was heavily furnished with plush carpeting, a plasma TV, high-end stereo system, and expensive artwork.

Cartier took a seat on the leather couch and continued to be silent. She had a lot to think about.

"We need to call my brother, Cartier. You know we need help on this. My *vatos* will be down."

"She already said she don't need your brother's help, so don't even bring it up again. I'm here. And together Cartier and I can handle this shit!"

"And what you plan to do, huh? You don't even know this fuckin' city.

This is my town — I run shit here. *Estamos dispuestos a matar mierda.*"

"Speak English, please. I don't understand that crazy tongue-twisting shit."

"I said, we are ready to kill shit." Quinn exhaled. "We take care of our own in Miami."

"This is how you take care of your own? By letting my homegirl's family get murdered and her daughter kidnapped? Whatever. The way we do shit back in Brooklyn—"

"This ain't fuckin' Brooklyn, Li'l Mama. This is Miami. Shit gets real down here."

"And we don't get fuckin' real in New York? Bitch, you better recognize who the fuck I am. Me and Cartier ran shit up top. Best believe that shit, bitch!" Li'l Mama said, slapping her hands together. She glared at Quinn. "Matter of fact, why is this bitch a fuckin' factor, Cartier? She ain't one of us. Why she in ya fuckin' circle? Ain't no fuckin' trust to outsiders."

Quinn glared back. She'd known Li'l Mama for less than a day and was ready to punch her in the face and fuck her up.

"Anyway, Cartier, let me contact some of our peoples back home and see if they can rustle up some cash for this fuckin' ransom. And then I can get on the phone with my man, Black Caesar, and tell him gather up some goons to bring down here, so we can shoot this fuckin' place up. You know I love Christian; she's like a daughter to me too. I'll burn this fuckin' place down to find her."

Quinn spat, "And that would be stupid. Any unnecessary drama by outsiders would bring heat."

"Bitch! I'm tired of you tryin' to play like you're the voice of reason and authority—like you runnin' shit."

"I do run shit, and if you haven't heard, I got three dozen vatos that would tell you the same. Who you got? An irrelevant dude named Black Caesar? You're a joke."

"Enough!" Cartier screamed.

The two girls looked at their mutual friend.

Cartier lifted herself from off the couch. "You think this shit wit' y'all is fuckin' helping me?"

"Cartier, you know I'm here for you," Li'l Mama said. "You can trust me."

"I don't know who to trust anymore."

"Cartier, you done bumped ya fuckin' head if you're implying you can't trust me. I know you're fucked up, but you ain't stupid."

Li'l Mama was hurt. After all she'd done for Cartier throughout the years she still hadn't earned her trust? But then she remembered how paranoid Cartier had always been, and rightfully so. Monya, who was Cartier's closest friend, and one of the founding members of the Cartel, had slept with her husband, Jason and had his son, Jason Jr. And Bam, also a founding member, had tried to have Cartier murdered, which ultimately ended up in her daughter Christian being shot. Li'l Mama decided not to take it personally. Especially at a time when Cartier needed her most.

"It's ya world, Cartier," Quinn said. "How you wanna play this out?"

"I don't know. I just want Christian back, at any cost. My daughter's life is at stake, so we gotta be careful. I can't risk anyone coming down here from New York, Li'l Mama."

"What about Head? Do you think he could help out in any way? If only for counsel?"

Cartier hadn't heard that name in months. She remembered her promise to him right after she recovered from her bullet wounds. She promised that she would never leave him while he did his bid, as his ex-girlfriend Tawana had. She also promised that she wouldn't miss one visit. She made a lot of promises that she didn't keep. Back then Cartier thought she would marry him, and that once he got out, they would live happily ever after. But that was that fairy tale fantasy life — that wasn't real. Those visits heading up North in a cold van with other women. Getting up at the crack of dawn and sitting in cold visiting rooms eating stale potato chips and vending-machine hamburgers.

Writing letters and doing visits became a full-time job, and Cartier didn't feel qualified. She was still young and didn't want to throw her last youthful years away traveling in and out of prisons for a man she wasn't really sure she loved. Each day that ticked by, she'd had more second thoughts. What if Head was just a rebound nigga? Loving arms to get her through the drama her husband — the real love of her life — had put her through? That doubt grew stronger and stronger, which caused her to drift farther and farther away.

At first she started not picking up all his calls. And when she would visit him he would be beefing. He'd told her that she wouldn't be around much longer, and she'd looked directly into his eyes and told him she would. Next, she'd stopped going on visits all together. Last, she'd stopped writing, and also reading his letters. She couldn't say she stopped sending him commissary money because she never had to. Head had his own paper. Cartier, at this moment, had to admit that she'd handled things like a grimy bitch. It was her fault her husband got murdered. And also her fault Head was locked down. And yet, up until twenty-four hours ago, she was living without a care in the world.

Cartier didn't know what to say. She hadn't told Li'l Mama that she was no longer in communication with Head. "I can't contact Head for support. I feel they watchin' us and know our every move."

"So what? We supposed to just stay here and not do shit?" Li'l Mama asked.

Cartier didn't respond. Her mind was racing with so many things.

Quinn left the room, leaving the two alone.

Cartier said to Li'l Mama, "I gotta call Janet."

"I know."

Cartier knew the news would crush Janet, who was like a second mother to her. Her mother's best friend was always by her side. And with Trina in critical condition, it was going to be devastating news.

"You want me to make the phone call?" Li'l Mama asked.

"No, I'll do it." Cartier reached for her cell phone and then tossed it back down. The situation was too overwhelming. "How do I grieve for my two sisters while having faith that my mother will pull through, and also keep a clear enough mind to come up with a strategy to get my daughter back? Any one of those situations is enough to break the strongest person. I got less than six days to make a move, and this situation is so heavy my feet feel firmly planted in cement."

"If you can't move" — Li'l Mama got down on both knees and grabbed both of Cartier's hands, "Then I will carry you! We have to get our little girl back. Trina is strong and can take care of herself. And I know it's fucked up about Fendi and Prada, but God has them. They're angels. And to keep it real, you can't bring them back."

The two friends shared a moment. It was just the push Cartier needed to focus on Christian.

CHAPTER 5

The next day, Cartier informed the girls that she had a little over two hundred thousand liquid to put toward the one-million-dollar ransom. It wouldn't even put a dent in it. She tried not to panic, but time was going by fast. She needed some big money, and she needed it fast.

"I only got five thousand on me," Li'l Mama said.

"And I have about nine thousand, but that ain't shit."

"What the fuck we gonna do?" Cartier asked in a panic. "They gonna kill my little girl."

"They ain't gonna fuckin' touch her. Listen, I have a plan. I know where we can get the money." Quinn had the undivided attention of both girls.

"Where?" Li'l Mama asked, eyeing Quinn suspiciously.

"Rico."

"Who the fuck is Rico?" Li'l Mama asked. "And why would he lend us that kind of cash?"

Quinn smirked. "Who said anything about him lending it to us?"

Cartier and Li'l Mama caught on quickly.

Unbeknownst to Cartier and Li'l Mama, Quinn would set up and rob drug dealers all around Miami. And she did it without her brother's knowledge or the gang's approval. She knew it was a dangerous trade, but it was also profitable.

Quinn excused herself, then walked back into the room carrying a small black duffel bag. She dropped it on the table. Cartier and Li'l Mama stared at it, puzzled. Quinn's face frowned as she unzipped the bag and revealed its contents. One by one, she began moving pistols and placing them on the table. When she was done, displayed in front of the girls was a small arsenal of weapons — several 9mms, a few Smith & Wessons, a .357, two .45s, and her favorite — a chrome Desert Eagle with a black grip.

The girls were silent, until Li'l Mama uttered, "Damn!"

"What I do is take what I need."

"You a stickup bitch," Li'l Mama said.

"You see that table, ay?" Quinn pointed to the pistols scattered across the glass dining room table. "We go in knockin' wit' those 'n' come back out wit' what we need."

"You serious?" Li'l Mama asked. "You would do this for Cartier?"

"What choice do we have? I been scopin' out Rico for a moment. I planned on movin' in on him in a few weeks, but now is a better time than ever. It's gonna be risky, 'cuz I don't know all his movements yet, but that *puto* can definitely get got."

Cartier was in deep thought.

Li'l Mama asked, "What you think, Cartier?"

Cartier frowned. She stared at Li'l Mama and then looked at Quinn. "I'm down fo' anything."

Quinn smiled.

"She down, I'm down," Li'l Mama said.

Knowing what they were about to get into made Cartier break down in tears. She thought she'd left this type of lifestyle behind in Brooklyn, but she couldn't seem to escape it.

Li'l Mama walked over to her friend to console her. She hugged Cartier closely. "We gonna be good, Cartier. You and me, we been through worse.

And Christian is comin' back home, you hear me? We gonna find her." She added, "Cartier, I vow, just like how I murdered Bam for her fuckin' betrayal against us — and she was peoples for almost twenty years — I'll slowly fuckin' murder whoever is involved wit' this shit. They gonna pay — wit' their lives. I don't give a fuck who it is."

Quinn and Li'l Mama locked eyes with each other. Their hard stares spoke volumes to each other. There was definitely some tension between the two.

Quinn picked up a 9mm and slammed a loaded clip into the pistol. "The same goes wit' me too." She cocked the hammer back, smirking at Li'l Mama while doing so. "Just tell me what I need to do, and I will play my position."

Cartier looked at her friends and knew she had to take charge. They were both bosses in their own right, but not like Cartier. She knew that Indians need a chief, and if they were going to successfully go after this mark, then it was going to take planning, because Cartier wouldn't be any good to Christian if she were dead. They would need to plan this jux all the way to the end, expect the unexpected, and be prepared to leave all cards on the table.

"So, Quinn, how much paper we talking 'bout?" Cartier rose to her feet, and suddenly the other two women recognized a formidable ally. The grief-stricken nervous wreck transformed into someone with purpose, motivation, and drive.

"He rollin' wit' at least half a millie or more."

"Is that liquid or weight?"

"That's all greenbacks, for sure." Quinn stepped closer to Cartier, appreciating the attention she was receiving.

Li'l Mama chimed in, "Are we running up in a stash house or his crib?"

Quinn walked over to her minibar and began pouring three glasses of Hennessey on the rocks. She figured they all needed to take the edge off.

"Stash house. There will be tons of cocaine and heroin, but we need to be in and out, right?" She handed Cartier the first glass, and then Li'l Mama.

"If it's sweet, then we take. In that moment, we're takers. Period." Cartier took a sip of the Henny. "But if for any reason shit is getting thick, then we grab the money and make a clean exit."

"Could any of this be traced back to you?" Li'l Mama asked Quinn.

Cartier answered, "If we're not careful it could be traced back to all of us. Not one of us is exempt from not only the heat coming around the corner to lock all our asses up but also retaliation. Down here there's a lot of gang affiliation. In order for us to successfully get away with these capers — two taps to the back of the head, close range. Clean. You feel me?"

Both women nodded their heads. Both understood there wasn't going to be just a *robbery, nobody gets hurt* type of situation. They were going in to take lives, along with anything of value, and if caught, they would surely not walk the street as free women ever again.

CHAPTER 6

Hector sat on the throne of the gang's clubhouse like the king he was, as Rick Ross's "Bag of Money" blared throughout the place. He took a few puffs from the large cigar clenched between his lips as he admired the scantily clad women dancing provocatively in front of him. The two tanned whores with long dark hair, wearing tight, coochie-cutting shorts and flimsy bikini tops, were grinding against each other and locking lips at the same time. The salacious scene made him release a devilish grin.

Surrounded by his goons, the Ghost Ridas, he felt untouchable. His two pit bull terriers were chained in the corner of the club, looking vicious and salivating. Their boisterous barks matched their ferocious bites. Mexican-born Hector loved his dogs. He wanted to be the Scarface of Miami. His notorious reputation ran throughout the city like a hurricane. Miami knew not to fuck with him.

The Ghost Ridas were in the clubhouse drinking and mingling with the ladies in the place. It was a full-fledged party in the wee hours of the morning. Some of the members began kissing and fondling the girls present, indicating an orgy was about to take place.

Hector took a swig from his beer and signaled for one of the scantily clad girls to come over to him. He then took another pull from his cigar.

The dark-haired beauty smiled and strutted over to him in her clear stilettos, her impish smile indicating that she was willing to do whatever he asked of her. She took a seat on Hector's lap.

Hector wrapped his arm around her slim waist and began massaging her thigh. "What's ya name?" he asked.

"Lilly," she said, smiling.

"Lilly, huh. I like that, ay."

"And I like you," she replied good-naturedly.

Hector passed her the beer he had in his hand, and she took a sip. Lilly then eyed the Mexican thug. She liked what she saw. Hector was boss. His bad-boy gangster image was a definite turn-on.

Unusually tall for his bloodline, handsome, and muscular, eighty percent of Hector's body was tatted up with gang tattoos and symbols, and raw sexual images. Scrawled on his back in big, bold ink was "666 Gangland, Devil's Disciple," and on his broad chest, "Ghost Ridas 4 Life." His heavily tattooed arms were impressive, and his cold, dark eyes indicated a killer and a leader.

Despite his thug image, Hector was also a well-dressed man. He always had a low, fresh-tapered haircut and loved to walk around in tailored black suits with a purple bandanna folded in his front breast pocket, Ferragamo shoes, and expensive watches. He believed that if you dressed the part of success then you could be the part.

Hector sat on the throne of the empire ready to take his crew to a whole new level. He wanted to control the streets, and was willing to invest in something much larger than the eyes could see.

Little Havana, and many parts of Miami, especially the south side, were the Ghost Ridas' playground. Their primary source of income was crystal meth, and with meth labs throughout Miami, the potent drug provided a sizeable income for the gang, netting anywhere from forty to ninety thousand a week in drug sales. They were ruthless killers, and they would constantly tag their gang signs all around Miami-Dade County to mark their territory. The majority of the members cared more about their murder game and street reputation than getting money. Their numbers were growing and growing fast, so they had become a major headache for the local authorities in South Beach.

The Ghost Ridas had been founded by Hector's older brother, Ricardo, who was a fierce figure in Miami. The stories about Ricardo's deadly temper were endless. He was known to have beaten a man to death with a hammer, repeatedly striking him in the face with it until the handle broke off and the man's face looked like ground beef. Then he drowned a man in the bathtub with the man's family watching.

Then there was another story about a couple affiliated with a rival gang that tried, unsuccessfully, to set Hector up to be killed. Ricardo was determined to make them pay. One night, he tracked them down to their home, and for hours, he and his crew tortured the couple, one member raping the female. And then Ricardo did the unthinkable. He cut off the boyfriend's dick with a razor and then stuffed it into the girlfriend's mouth, making her suck on it at first and then choking her with the severed penis, ramming it down her throat until she couldn't breathe any more.

Ricardo was murdered ten years ago, when Hector was only fifteen. He was gunned down in the passenger seat of an idling Cadillac. Ricardo was betrayed by a once-loyal soldier. Hector took his brother's place and continued his violent ways. Now, the Ghost Ridas were almost ten thousand strong and spreading throughout the North and Southeastern states.

Hector continued to fondle the girl. Her smooth skin felt like silk. Her smile turned him on, and her touch was making his dick hard. He looked over at his right-hand, Tumble, who was mingling with a few scantily clad whores.

"I want to kiss your dick," the girl whispered, seductively.

Hector smiled. She stood up with Hector's hand in hers, ready to lead him into one of the private backrooms in the clubhouse.

Hector took one final pull from the burning cigar between his lips and put it out against the wall. "You sure ya ready for this?"

"Let's go find out," she said, beaming.

They started off toward the room, but Hector soon noticed Stone entering the clubhouse with a troubled expression. Stone was a ruthless nineteen-year-old *vato* whom Hector had taken under his wing.

Stone went up to Tumble and whispered something in his ear. Whatever it was he'd said to Tumble, his reaction didn't look good.

Tumble looked over at Hector, and the two locked eyes. Tumble started to make his way over toward Hector.

The young whore asked Hector, "You comin'?"

"Wait the fuck up!" he snapped.

The young whore knew not to push her boundaries, so she stood next to the towering thug. But Hector didn't want her in his business. He nudged her off the raised platform and said, "Give us a fuckin' minute."

She didn't argue with him.

"What up, yo?" Hector asked Tumble.

"Young homie just came to me wit' some serious news, ay."

"About what?"

"Some serious one-eighty-seven shit went down at Cartier's place. Ain't that Quinn's people?"

Hector nodded. "What the fuck happened? She dead?"

"Not her, but I just heard her family's been wiped out."

Hector had been salivating over Cartier ever since she'd arrived in Miami and linked up with his sister Quinn. Her Brooklyn edginess had immediately caught his eye. He would have done anything to be with her, but he wasn't her type. Cartier was used to being with a Brooklyn thug that had a certain amount of swagger and slick talk. Besides, she already had Head back in New York, and even though he was locked down, she wasn't ready to commit to a new relationship.

Hearing the news put Hector in a bad place. He asked Tumble, "You know who's responsible?"

"Nah."

"Where is she now?"

"My guess, probably wit' ya sister."

"Find my sister, then. And find out who was behind this shit."

Hector stood stationary among his crew, serious thoughts spinning through his head. Even though Cartier wasn't a gang member or family, he still had some kind of affinity for her. He respected her style, hustle, and courage, and knew that a bitch like her wasn't going to take her family's murder lying down. Wanting to impress her, he was ready to take it to the streets and, if possible, find out who was responsible for the butchery of her family. He was ready to spread blood for Cartier.

Hector looked over at the young female waiting patiently for him. She smiled, but he didn't smile back. More urgent matters now had his attention. He suddenly dismissed her like she was a nuisance, leaving a bitter expression on her face. Hector went into one of the back rooms alone, where he closed the door behind him and sat in a massive leather chair, thinking.

❧❦ CHAPTER 7 ❦❧

Every hour that went by made Cartier more uneasy. She had a very small window of time in which to hustle one million dollars for her daughter's ransom, and she had less than a quarter of the money on hand. Though the feat seemed impossible, Quinn had advised them of a sure thing, and Cartier was desperate enough to try anything.

All three ladies, dressed as if they were going to a South Beach club, got into the black truck, but partying was the last thing on their minds. Cartier couldn't stop thinking about her daughter. The thought of Christian, so young and so innocent, in the hands of monsters had her seething.

It was a late and balmy evening. The night's temperature had reached eighty degrees, and the sky was cluttered with stars that seemed to be raining down on the city.

Cartier rode in the backseat silently, her .380 holstered on her thigh, while Quinn drove. Li'l Mama rode shotgun, pulling on a Kush blunt. She exhaled and passed the blunt back to Cartier.

"Here, take a hit of that," Li'l Mama said to her.

Cartier declined. She wasn't in the mood to get high. She remained aloof as weed smoke fogged up the truck. She gripped her cell phone, hoping it would ring, and that her daughter's kidnappers would let her speak to Christian. She just wanted to hear her voice, to tell her baby that she loved her, and that Mama was coming for her. But her cell phone remained silent.

"Don't worry, Cartier, we gonna do this right an' get that money up."

"I swear, Quinn," Li'l Mama said, "nothin' better not go wrong."

"If you don't fuck up, it'll go down smooth," Quinn replied.

Li'l Mama sighed and sat back. Quinn's plan was going to take skilled acting and some luck. The girls looked highbrow in their intoxicating, expensive dresses. Cartier wore a black Givenchy dress in a style that Rihanna had once worn on the cover of GQ Magazine. The dress left almost nothing to the imagination. Quinn sported a tantalizing lace dress with a low-cut neckline, and Li'l Mama wore a classic white, short-sleeve minidress.

Quinn continued to navigate her truck toward their destination; Rico's main stash house in Liberty City. She felt like they had two things going for them: their sex appeal and the fact that niggas assumed that women were the inferior sex.

"There they go, right there," Quinn said.

Li'l Mama and Cartier turned to take notice.

Quinn stopped her truck at the end of the block and watched the activity in front of Rico's stash house; a well-kept, one-family home with a small porch and a slanted stucco rooftop, a short iron gate, and a paved driveway. A few soldiers were lingering out front, smoking and gambling.

Cartier stared at the home. "How much you say is inside?" she asked.

"He a serious dope boy down hurr, so I say 'bout half a million, maybe much, much more."

Cartier wouldn't have given a fuck if Quinn had said ten large. For every dollar she could hustle up to get back Christian, she was down.

"Ante up, then," Cartier chimed, cocking back the hammer to her .380.

The ladies decided to put their plan into action.

Quinn parked the truck a few blocks from the spot, and they all stepped out. The three ladies lingered outside their truck, their hearts racing. It was going to be a dramatic moment. Things had to look real. They had to look like victims. They had to come off as weak, docile, and nonthreatening to their targets.

Quinn stared at Li'l Mama. She was a new face, so she was the one that had to do the acting. "You ready fo' this?" she asked Li'l Mama.

"You just make sure you don't fuck me up," Li'l Mama said.

"I'm sorry," Quinn said.

"No, ya not." Li'l Mama braced herself.

Quinn slightly ripped the edge of Li'l Mama's dress and then hit her with the pistol, all part of the plan.

Li'l Mama cringed and scowled, blood coming from her forehead. It was a hard blow, made to look authentic. The blood would provide authenticity in the storytelling, and the theatrical performance would be the follow-up. Li'l Mama was ready to play ball.

Cartier tore her own dress a little. The thought of her missing daughter brought her to tears, which was perfect. She glanced at Quinn, trusting that the scheme would work.

They watched the block and finally saw Rico turn his silver 550 Benz into the driveway of his stash house. He was quickly greeted by his workers and goons as he stepped out, looking dapper in a black velour tracksuit and wearing lots of jewelry, Gucci shades concealing his eyes, throwback Gucci sneakers on his feet.

"There he go," Quinn said. "Fuck it! Rock out!"

The two girls went off running frantically, screaming and looking horrified.

"Help us! Help us!" Li'l Mama screamed as the two women ran toward Rico's stash house. Cartier was running behind her with one shoe on, the other clutched in her hand.

They instantly caught the attention of Rico and his hustlers. Activity on the block stopped as the two fly females in distress approached the house.

"What the fuck!" Rico exclaimed, his eyes glued to the two women.

"They robbed us!" Li'l Mama screamed. "They took our ride!"

Rico kept his hand near his concealed 9mm, not knowing what to expect. His shifty eyes darted around quickly. When he saw the blood trickling from Li'l Mama's forehead, his apprehension eased, slightly.

Cartier shouted, "Someone call the police! Call the cops!"

"Whoa, whoa! Y'all ladies, chill fo' a moment," Rico said. The inflection in his voice demanding respect.

"No, they took my shit!" Li'l Mama screamed. "They took my fuckin' ride!"

"Who took ya shit?" Rico asked.

"I don't fuckin' know. They fuckin' carjacked us. They hurt my friend. She's up the block."

Rico knew he couldn't have police in front of his stash house. His operation was quiet, and under the radar, so calling the police for a carjacking situation with three females — one being injured, was absolutely out of the question.

"Nah, no police," he said calmly. "Not on this block."

"I want my shit back!" Li'l Mama yelled.

"Yo, y'all niggas, go see about her friend," Rico instructed his thugs.

Two men quickly went up the block, and a short moment later, one was carrying Quinn, who looked disoriented and hurt.

"What the fuck happened to her?" Rico asked the girls.

"They pistol-whipped me and snatched me outta my fuckin' Beamer." Li'l Mama sounded hysterical, tears streaming down her eyes and blood still trickling from her forehead.

"Yo, sorry 'bout that, but I can have my peoples take you home an' you can call the cops from there. Tell 'em what happened."

"I need to make a phone call. Ohmygod, I can't believe this fuckin' shit happened to me. Ohmygod! Ohmygod! I can't believe this fuckin' shit! This ain't fuckin' happenin'. They took my fuckin' BMW!"

Rico looked around and saw his neighbors looking at the situation. The females were already stirring up unwanted attention with their disheveled look and the screaming hysterics.

"Yo, Miles, take them inside, have 'em make a phone call, get them cleaned up but then they gotta bounce," Rico said.

Miles nodded. So far, everything was playing out perfectly for the girls. They followed Miles, a dark-skinned young male with two long ponytails. He was born and raised in Mississippi, and had moved farther south three years ago and linked up with Rico and his get-money thugs.

Once they were inside the house, Cartier immediately began scoping out the scene. The place was sparsely furnished, with two leather couches, a flat-screen, chairs, and shaky tables. Two males were on the couch engaged in a shoot-'em-up Xbox game and smoking weed while loud rap music was playing. And with a few guns on display, the place screamed drug stash house.

The ladies caught the males' attention, so they put their game on pause.

"Fellows, we have some guests," Rico said coolly. "Let's make these beautiful ladies feel at home. They had an unfortunate situation."

Quinn, Li'l Mama, and Cartier stood in the center of the living room. They seemed to be nervous. Li'l Mama was still in tears, putting on a stellar performance.

In total, there were five men in the house, including Rico. The girls had to be methodical because they were outnumbered and definitely outgunned. But the men, smitten by their beauty and curvy figures, had made the grave mistake of assuming that the ladies were helpless victims.

Rico said to them, "Ladies, *mi casa*, your *casa*. Y'all can get comfortable, an' we gonna get ya situation taken care of." He gestured for them to have a seat somewhere.

"What we gonna do about my fucking BMW?" Li'l Mama continued.

"What model you had, ma?"

"Huh?"

"Your car. You keep screamin' that you had a poor man's whip that got jacked. I'm gonna put my niggas on the case, but they can't find what they don't know they're looking for."

"Oh." Li'l Mama rolled her eyes. "I had a black .325."

"Damnnnnn," Rico joked. "You too fine to be actin' all brand-new over a .325 BMW. Our girls don't drive anything less than the hottest whips, Audi R-9s, Ranges and Benzes. Tonight could be your lucky night after all."

"Really? How so?" Cartier piped in.

"If any one of y'all play your cards right there could be an upgrade in your future."

"We all only date bosses, and it seems to me there's only one in here." Cartier ran her hands down her voluptuous hips, and then continued, "So does that mean we all gonna get a new whip?"

Cartier was being facetious, which caught Rico's attention.

"I like the way homegirl talking. Why don't y'all ladies make yourself comfortable? Get to know me and my niggas."

"First let me wash my fuckin' face," Li'l Mama said to him.

"Bathroom's down the hall." Rico pointed the way. "Last door to ya right."

Li'l Mama went to the bathroom and closed the door behind her. She flicked on the lights and stared at her reflection in the mirror. She was ready to punch Quinn in the face, but she knew the injury had to look real. "Damn! I hope this shit don't fuckin' scar," she said, nursing the small wound to her head.

She cleaned herself up, splashing water on her face and hyping herself up to do the robbery. She removed the .45 from her small purse and checked the clip. It was ready for action. *Niggas is so fuckin' stupid*, she thought. It was like the wooden horse being led into the gates of Troy, except this time it was tits and ass that turned the men into idiots.

Li'l Mama remained in the bathroom for a few minutes. She had to be fast when the time came. She took a deep breath, put the pistol back into her purse, and exited the bathroom looking a little bit calmer.

"You okay?" Rico asked her when she returned from the bathroom.

She nodded.

Quinn and Cartier were seated with the two Xbox players, who seemed to have found something a lot more interesting than the video game.

"Anything y'all need, I got that. But this is my hood, and anything that goes down, I'll get to the bottom of it. And I'm gonna make it my personal business to find the niggas that carjacked you." Rico went into his pockets and pulled out a wad of bills. He peeled off a few hundreds and passed it to Li'l Mama, who looked confused.

"Take it. I'm the authority now," he said. "I know you want to involve the police. But check it, y'all ain't get jacked around here. I don't need that attention around my business."

Li'l Mama hissed, "But my car —"

"I'ma find ya car. Y'all just chill and get ya drink on. Y'all in good hands right now."

The ladies looked reluctant at first. The strong gleam in the men's eyes told them that they were looking for much more than some conversation and a smile. Suddenly, they felt like prey among wolves.

"We good?" Rico asked.

Li'l Mama nodded, and Rico smiled.

Soon, the girls partook in weed smoking and drinking. The fellows foolishly thought they were manipulating their guests.

Before long, the girls separated the men. Li'l Mama went into the master bedroom with Rico. Quinn had two of her own to entertain, as did Cartier.

Rico was ready to have his way with Li'l Mama in the dimmed room. She wanted him to strip naked, but he wasn't too keen on shedding his clothing before he could see his prize in the buff also. Before he could fondle Li'l Mama, she subtly removed the pistol that she had concealed inside her purse and struck him over the head with the barrel.

Rico stumbled back. "What the fuck!" When he got his composure, he was staring down the barrel of a .45.

"I can easily make this shit into a one-eighty-seven," Li'l Mama snarled.

"Bitch, you crazy!"

"Strip!" she ordered through clenched teeth.

Rico glared at her, but Li'l Mama's eyes told him she wasn't a rookie at this. He slowly began to remove his clothing. "You have the audacity to rob me, bitch?"

Li'l Mama didn't respond. She went searching through his room and found a loaded SIG .9 hidden under the pillows.

"You can never be too careful," she said.

She then forced Rico back into the living room, where her two accomplices had their men on their knees at gunpoint.

Cartier removed duct tape from her pocketbook and bound their wrists and ankles and then placed it over the men's mouths, except for Rico's.

"Y'all bitches are dead! You fuckin' hear me?" Rico exclaimed. "Dead!"

Cartier stepped up behind him and pushed the barrel of the .380 to the back of his head. "You have two options. Either give up the money and live, or don't, and die."

"Fuck you!"

"Wrong answer." Cartier turned the gun downward and shot him in the back of the knee.

Rico screamed out, wincing and squirming from the pain. The blood from the gunshot wound started to stain the carpet.

Cartier told him, "Next time, a bullet's gonna penetrate a much more vital area."

Rico doubled over, his wrists bound behind him, and landed on his side. He continued screaming.

Cartier stood over him, the gun aimed at him. "We gonna ask you again."

The other men looked on, their eyes becoming wide with fear, mumbling incoherently underneath the duct tape. The ladies were in complete control. Quinn watched the door, and Li'l Mama was ready to become extremely violent.

"Where is everything?" Cartier demanded.

Rico stared up at Cartier with teary eyes.

She was becoming impatient. Cartier nodded toward Li'l Mama, and she quickly and randomly chose one of the goons and flipped him over, torso facing up. Cartier didn't hesitate to shoot one of Rico's men in the dick, and the young goon bellowed from the excruciating pain. His private area was quickly covered with a crimson stain as he squirmed around with his wrists still tied behind him.

"I ain't fuckin' playin, ya heard!" Cartier shouted.

"In the kitchen and first bedroom," Rico growled.

"Now, was that so fuckin' hard?"

Li'l Mama went into the rooms to get the stash. She then rushed back out with a black bag filled with cash and another small bag filled with drugs. "Let's go," she said.

Li'l Mama felt like nobody had to die tonight. They got what they came for and she hoped that Cartier would see it that way.

As the ladies were about to leave, only Cartier lingered behind. She knew that Li'l Mama and Quinn were ready to disregard her orders: two shots to the back of the head. Clean.

While she took a moment to clear her thoughts, Rico helped make up her mind when he shouted, "You fucked up robbin' me, bitch! You have no idea what y'all done! You fuckin' hear me? I will hunt you bitches down an' not only touch you, but I swear, I'll touch an' destroy everything that y'all love."

Cartier's face tightened with a disturbing scowl. She glared at Rico like a madwoman. She wasn't going to take his threat lightly. She walked over to him and, without a second thought, put two bullets into the back of his head, dropping him face-down. In succession, Li'l Mama and Quinn followed suit, killing everyone inside, leaving behind no witnesses or any further threats to themselves.

"Look, anything we touched, we get rid of or wipe down," Cartier said.

They tossed bottles and glasses that might have had their fingerprints on them into a black trash bag and wiped down the areas they thought they'd touched. When they were sure everything was cleaned, the ladies rushed out of the home and hurriedly moved up the block toward their parked vehicle, their adrenaline pumping fast.

Quinn jumped behind the wheel of the truck and sped off, tires screeching. It was a successful score, but a bloody mess. Neither woman had any regrets about the bodies they'd left behind. It was their world, the lives they'd chosen, and their way of doing business.

As Quinn sped toward the highway, Cartier sat in the backseat wondering, *Did I fuck up somewhere in the past?* She thought that maybe she'd gotten into a beef with someone and left them alive to avenge the infraction. She vowed she would never make a mistake like that again. She knew if she and her daughter survived this, then she would have to leave Miami, plant roots in a different state again, maybe California, because after this bloodbath, Miami was no longer safe for her and Christian.

CHAPTER 8

Detectives Lam and Sharp stood over the five bodies in the house, clad in their fine suits and wearing latex gloves. Sharp shook his head in disbelief. It was going to be another long night for them both. The dark blood on the floor had pooled around the dead men, and the place reeked of decomposing bodies. Cops flooded every square inch of the house, and nosy neighbors stood huddled next to each other outside the home, behind the yellow police tape, onlookers to another murderous crime scene in Miami-Dade.

"This city is hell," Detective Sharp said to his partner, staring intently at the five dead men before his feet.

"Seems like our boy Rico finally met with a bigger and more dangerous wolf," Detective Lam said lightheartedly. Honestly, he really didn't give a fuck about five murdered dope dealers.

Sharp released a heavy sigh. He crouched near Rico and stared at the body, as if Rico would get up and whisper to him the culprits behind his violent demise. "Who did this to you, huh?"

Detective Lam started to inspect the other dead men. With their wrists tied behind their backs and lying face-down, it indicated a home invasion that was well planned.

"What you think, partner?" Lam asked.

"I say maybe two or three perpetrators. Maybe they knew their killers," Sharp replied.

Detective Lam looked at his partner and smiled. "So you think maybe one of the workers got greedy and wanted to take it all?" he asked in disbelief.

"It's the only way I can see this happening. Trust had a hand in this. How many times do we lock up family members or best friends for murdering over money? And you see there isn't any sign of forced entry."

Lam nodded.

Detective Sharp started to roam through the house, his trained eyes taking in everything. He focused on the kitchen countertop then shifted his eyes toward the tiled floor, where he saw something that could contradict his theory — a woman's diamond earring underneath the kitchen table. He picked it up with his latex gloves and observed that it had layers of dust on it before displaying it to his partner.

"What you got?" Detective Lam uttered.

"A woman's earring. From the looks of it, it must have gotten lost long ago. But, you never know."

"Bag it as evidence then." Detective Lam stated. "You never know, she could have been a witness."

"Or participant."

"That too."

The coroners had arrived with multiple body bags to fill, and CSI was heavily probing any additional physical evidence left behind.

"I need some air," Lam said.

"I'll join you."

The two detectives exited the house and stood on the porch. Authority figures came and went from the home. Lam lit up a cigarette and observed his surroundings. There were so many eyes watching them. The neighbors whispered, looked. But there was a strong wall of community silence that was difficult for the officers to break through. Fear and intimidation kept killers free, and as a result, the poorest communities became a haven for the drug dealers.

Detective Sharp stared at all the onlookers watching them from behind the yellow crime-scene tape. He knew someone out there knew something, but the trick was getting a witness to talk. Rico was a well-known man in the hood, liked by most, but hated by many. He had his hands in a few murders himself, and this was definitely karma coming back at him.

"So what you think?" Lam said. "Someone had to see something. Too many faces around for these killers to go unnoticed."

"They won't talk. They fear them more than they fear us."

Just then, a tricked-out Impala with dark tints, candy paint, and chrome wheels came to a screeching stop on the block. The driver and passenger doors flew open, and two men rushed out with intense grimaces on their face. It was obvious they were kin or friends to the victims inside.

"What the fuck, yo! What the fuck!" one of the men screamed. He stood about six-two and was wearing a Miami Heat, LeBron James jersey. His menacing dark features were twisted with rage. He sported a gleaming bald head, and tattoos ran up and down his muscular arms — he had killer/goon written all over him.

His partner, the passenger, was just as tall with 360-degree waves on his low-cut Caesar and cold eyes. He was black as night, shirtless, and in dark, sagging jeans, his upper body swathed with tattoos, gang symbols scrawled across his neck. His biceps flexed as he tried to push his way past the police officers shielding the crime scene.

"Yo, get the fuck off me! That's my cousin's crib, yo!" the man shouted. "What the fuck happened?"

Half a dozen cops tried to stop the two men from rushing past them and into the home. A scuffle ensued, and the two men were quickly restrained.

"Calm the fuck down!" one of the officers yelled.

"Fuck y'all!"

Both men were thrown against a parked car and quickly handcuffed. But they continued to curse and be disorderly.

Detectives Lam and Sharp rushed over to help.

"Listen, just relax and we can talk," Sharp said to them.

"Fuck that! Yo, who bodied my fuckin' cousin?" the shirtless man screamed.

"Who's your cousin?" Sharp asked.

"Rico!"

"I'm sorry about what happened inside," Sharp said softly. "My condolences to you and your family."

"I ain't trying to hear that shit, man!" he asked, almost choking in anguish. "Who killed him, man?"

"What's your name?"

"Bones."

The two men became calm after speaking with Sharp. He had a silver tongue.

Bones, unable to hide his grief, broke down in front of the officers. Though Rico was his first cousin, they had been like brothers.

"We would like to take you down to the station for questioning," Sharp asked him. "Just to see if you have any information that could lead to an arrest and conviction."

Bones was insulted. "What did you just say?"

Detective Sharp wasn't easily intimidated. "I said help us out!"

Bones swatted both detectives away as he and his partner decided to bounce.

Detective Lam called out, mockingly, "That's how you gonna rep your cousin? You just gonna walk off? His body ain't even cold yet in the morgue and you already forgotten him!"

Detective Sharp chimed in, "Don't you want justice? For Rico? Help us send his killer to jail."

Bones called over his shoulder, "I hold court in the streets, partner. Best believe that."

CHAPTER 9

The ladies didn't go to sleep after the robbery and homicide. The money stolen from Rico's place was poured out onto the dining-room table at Quinn's place and counted there. They only came off with two hundred and fifty thousand dollars and nine ki's of cocaine. It wasn't that much, but it was still something to put toward the ransom. Cartier was still short, and time was running out. The girls knew it wouldn't take long for word to travel. Rico was well known, and liked, too, so the girls had to remain low-key. But with Christian's life on the line, it was going to be difficult.

Cartier sat slouched on the couch, her cell phone glued to her hand. She desperately wanted it to ring. She needed to know something. She needed to hear from her daughter and her kidnappers, but there was nothing.

The tiredness and stress showed on the ladies' faces. Quinn lit up a cigarette and stared at TV. She prepared a second pot of coffee, hoping that the additional caffeine would help with stamina. Quinn hated to admit it, but a bitch was tired. All this robbery and kidnapping was enough to drain the most thorough hood bitch. In reality, she wanted to toss Cartier and Li'l Mama the fuck out her crib, close the blinds, and sleep in for two days straight. But she was brought up on the word "loyalty," and if she didn't do all she could to help out a homie in need, then it would get back to Hector. And she knew better than to get on her brother's bad side, especially knowing that he had a thing for Cartier.

Li'l Mama sat near Cartier, each woman consumed with her own worrying thoughts. Short several hundred grand for the ransom, there was the likelihood that maybe they wouldn't get the money, and Christian's fate was already sealed.

Out of the blue, a phone rang. Cartier jumped to look at hers, but it was silent. It was Quinn's phone. She looked at the screen before answering it. Quinn removed herself from the living room and went into one of the bedrooms to talk to her brother, Hector.

Li'l Mama stared after Quinn suspiciously, and when she was out of earshot, she said to Cartier, "I still don't trust this bitch. Why the fuck is she goin' to the extreme to help us out?"

"Li'l Mama, chill. I'm not in the fuckin' mood to hear you complain."

"Ain't nobody complaining." Li'l Mama frowned. "I just think we need to keep an eye on this husky bitch."

"What the fuck!" Cartier was about to implode. "I gotta keep an eye out for Quinn. Concentrate on raising enough dough to get my daughter back. Pray that my moms pulls through her surgery. And also, umm, let's see, prepare to lay my two baby sisters to rest. You sound like a fucking moron, Li'l Mama! Quinn just helped me come up off a quarter of a million dollars. What the fuck?!"

Li'l Mama was seething. She thought that Cartier would see what she saw—which was a sneaky bitch in Quinn. She was an original founding member of the Cartel, and thought she should have been shown more respect.

Li'l Mama grabbed a brush from her purse and began brushing her long hair until she placed it into a ponytail. Truth be told, she was ready to blow this joint. She was tired of Cartier and her ungrateful, smart mouth. Shit, if she wasn't needed then she could go back home.

"It's all good, Cartier. Every last drop." She stood up and walked out on the deck to get some air.

Cartier sighed, leaning her head back into the cushion and glancing at her phone again. She had her phone in one hand and her gun lying near her on the couch. She could hear Quinn in the other room talking. She felt like she couldn't move. The worry was overwhelming her.

Quinn walked into the living room looking cool as ice. "My brother's coming over," she said to Cartier.

"Why?"

"He heard what happened and wanna give his support."

Cartier didn't respond. She already knew Hector had a strong crush on her, but she wasn't interested in him at all, and now, especially during a catastrophic time in her life, she just wanted to disappear somewhere.

"I didn't tell him about Christian."

Cartier stayed remote. It was Quinn's place, not hers. So she couldn't dictate who could come over and who couldn't.

An hour later, a burgundy Escalade with 24-inch chrome rims came to a complete stop in front of Quinn's place. The doors opened, and Hector, Tumble, and a young thug named Monster stepped out of the truck.

Hector stood tall and looked like a powerful gangster in his wifebeater, flexing his muscles and ornate gang tattoos, his purple bandana hanging from his back pocket. A long platinum chain with a diamond cut pit-bull-head pendant hung from around his neck.

He took a pull from the long cigar clutched between his fingers then said to Tumble and Monster, "Y'all niggas stay out here. I'll be only a minute."

His two goons nodded and lingered by the truck with their bad-tempered frowns. The men seemed unapproachable and intimidating. Wearing a long Miami Dolphins jersey, Tumble leaned against the Escalade, his Glock 17 tucked into his waistband, his eyes dancing around the block, keeping an eye out for any trouble.

Quinn greeted her brother at the front door, giving him a loving hug and kiss. He walked into the home and saw Cartier seated on the couch smoking a blunt.

Cartier looked up at Hector and didn't say a word.

He walked over and said, "I heard what went down. My condolences. But best believe I'm gonna have my peoples all over this shit."

"Don't!"

"Why not?"

"'Cuz I don't need ya help, Hector. This is my problem."

"You bein' stubborn, Cartier. I can have my peoples all over this city lookin' fo' the people that did this shit."

Cartier stood up and glared at Hector. "Stay out my business, Hector. This doesn't concern you." Then she stormed off into one of the bedrooms and slammed the door behind her.

"*¿Qué demonios es su problema?*" Hector exclaimed, asking his sister in Spanish, "What the fuck is her problem?"

"Rough day for all of us," Quinn replied.

"Yeah? Well, when she feels like my help, call me. Anyway, you be careful out here. I just got word that Rico an' his crew was killed last night."

"Damn!"

"Yeah, five of 'em executed. Some say they got that nigga for a couple million and some heroin. Some say they got that nigga for a hundred large an' some ki's. Word is they got a lynching squad chasin' whoever is responsible."

Quinn pretended to be shocked by the news. She took a seat on the couch. "Ay, that's fucked up."

"It is. But you keep close. Any problems, you let me know, sis."

"Will do."

Hector hugged Quinn and walked out the place, leaving her with the feeling that she'd gotten away with murder. She went toward the window to watch him leave.

When he was gone, she went charging into the bedroom where Cartier had disappeared to. "Cartier, what the fuck is wrong wit' you? My brother is tryin' to help you. He really cares about you."

"I don't need his help," she spat.

"But you need my help though."

Cartier glared at her friend. "I can do this without you, too."

"No, you fuckin' can't." Quinn then softened her tone. "Look, I know this shit is fucked up, but we gonna find her. And we gonna get this money up fo' this ransom. And we gonna kill every last muthafucka that was behind this."

Cartier stared at her moms lying almost lifeless in the bed. The pain of seeing such a strong woman now looking so frail was excruciating. Tears welled up in her eyes as she stood over Trina's bed. The humming of the machines that kept her mother alive resonated throughout the room.

Trina might as well have been dead, though, because the doctors had stated that she was irreversibly brain dead. Her body lay rigid, her eyes remained shut, and her soul was gone. Connected to a ventilator and several tubes, including one for feeding and another for breathing, Trina looked like something out of *The Matrix*. And even though she was getting the best care at Jackson Memorial Hospital as they fought to keep her breathing and stable, they couldn't perform miracles. The inevitable had to happen — Cartier would have to pull the plug on her mother.

The scene was reminiscent of Monya. Back then, when Monya was in a coma, brain dead after being shot in her head, Cartier was in denial. She felt that Monya would make a miraculous recovery and rejoin the Cartel members. Each day that Monya lingered, clinging onto life, took an unhealthy toll on everyone; especially her mother, Janet. Cartier felt that Janet never fully recovered from her daughter's early demise. And rightfully so. No parent should ever have to bury their child.

Trina had died in that apartment, though. This was nothing but a shell of the mother she loved. Trina had fought, but the battle was lost. The damage to her body and to her skull was too extensive.

Cartier had already signed the papers, giving the doctors permission to pull the plug and end the agony. And she had already made the funeral arrangements for her family. Trina had the right to join her daughters in heaven, so it was only right to bury her mother along with her two sisters.

Tears continued to trickle down Cartier's grief-stricken face. She let loose a heavy sigh. She felt her breakdown coming near. Her daughter was missing, and her family was dead — it felt like hell on earth.

Cartier bent down and planted a kiss on her mother's pasty cheek as memories of better times came rushing back.

"I'm sorry, Ms. Timmons," the doctor said to her in a sad tone.

"Sorry? Fuck sorry! The people responsible behind this will be sorry a'ight," she said, staring at her mother.

The doctor looked confused by Cartier's statement. He started to jot down a few notes on his clipboard and then said to Cartier, "I know this is hard for you. And I recommend getting some emotional support for yourself after making this difficult decision. I suggest you talk with a professional counselor, a member of clergy, or even a good friend to get those feelings out in the open and begin to deal with them."

But Cartier wasn't listening to the doctor. His advice went in one ear and out the next. Her mind was far away, in a dangerous place. She didn't give a fuck about emotional support. She wanted revenge and her daughter back. She fixed her eyes on her mother and sadly uttered the words, "I love you."

"You're making the right decision," the doctor added.

"Just do the shit," Cartier spat. "Put her in a better place than here." She spun on her heels and left out the doorway.

Waiting outside the hospital in the Range Rover was Li'l Mama. Cartier dried her umpteenth tear for her mother before she climbed into the passenger seat with a hard expression.

Li'l Mama already knew the state she was in. She took a pull from the Newport and then flicked it out the window. She then looked at Cartier and said, "I know that was hard for you. She was a mother to me, too."

"I'ma fuckin' kill 'em all, Li'l Mama. I swear, I'ma rip whoever's behind this apart wit' my bare fuckin' hands." Cartier stared aimlessly at the windshield, distraught beyond belief. She didn't even bother to turn to look at her friend while she spoke. Her mind was plagued with so many horrors.

"And I'm right here wit' you, Cartier. I'm here. Let's fuckin' do this," Li'l Mama replied. "What now, though?"

"Shopping."

Li'l Mama looked puzzled. "Shopping?"

"Just drive. I got a plan."

Li'l Mama started the car and made her way out the parking spot, headed toward the nearest shopping district.

Cartier lit a blunt and glanced at her cell phone, which hadn't rung for a minute. As the deadline approached, she became even more nervous. But Cartier refused to become some patsy. It was time to hunt and kill.

Fearing her phone might be tapped, Cartier went into a MetroPCS store and purchased a few throwaway phones. She couldn't chance talking on her own phone. The only time it would be used was if the kidnappers called.

Their next stop was to a car rental service. The ladies needed something a little more inconspicuous; the Range Rover had suddenly become too showy. Cartier sent Li'l Mama into the Hertz car rental near the airport because she didn't want her name on anything.

Cartier sat behind the steering wheel of the Range Rover and waited patiently for Li'l Mama to leave the lot with the rental car. She smoked a cigarette, her mind flooded with memories of her family, and thinking about her daughter.

Who to trust and who not to? she asked herself. If Cartier knew one thing as fact, it would be that this was a revenge murder/kidnapping. It had to be someone from her past. But who? And why? Perhaps even why now?

She knew her enemies were deadly, but what scared her most — she didn't know who the enemy was. An unseen foe was horrifying. And these people meant serious business. It could have been someone in her own camp or a disgruntled ally from her past.

Li'l Mama came rolling out the rental lot honking the horn of a clean black Dodge Avenger. Cartier started the ignition to the truck and followed Li'l Mama until they were far away from the rental place. The two then pulled over to the side of the road to talk.

Cartier stepped out of the truck and walked over to the Avenger. "Two things I need for you to do," she said. "One, get us a hotel room, someplace quiet and discreet." She no longer felt safe at Quinn's place.

Li'l Mama nodded.

"And two, I need you to contact Head for me. I need his resources on this one. See if he can look into who's the mastermind on this."

"I'm on it."

Cartier stepped away from the car but suddenly returned with an afterthought. "Oh, and contact Janet for me. She needs to know."

"It's gonna hit her hard," Li'l Mama replied sadly.

Cartier sighed. "I know."

It was something the girls had forgotten to do. Janet was like a mother to them. And it pained the two Brooklyn girls that someone had to deliver the heart-wrenching news to such a close friend.

Cartier climbed back into the Range Rover, and the two went their separate ways. Cartier left Quinn out of the plan, just in case. She was still a new piece to an intricate puzzle, and Cartier was paranoid and didn't know who to trust.

❋❆ CHAPTER 10 ❆❋

NEW YORK

"**O**oooh, fuck me, daddy! Fuck me!" Janet howled, feeling the young thug's big dick cram into her juicy pink folds while she fucked him in the cowgirl position.

She kneeled astride him and leaned forward on her arms, her hands pressed against his hairless chest, while he lay back, giving her control.

Electricity shot through Janet's body. Her pussy began to throb and pulse, getting wetter with each stroke. His dick was magnetic. Without saying a word, she lowered her breast into his waiting mouth. He rose up a little while still thrusting vigorous strokes into her and started sucking on her fleshy breast as his hands began to caress her curves.

"Mmmm, that feels so nice," she cooed, bouncing on top of him. "Don't stop. Oh, yeah, feel my tits. Lick them melons, baby."

Janet leaned deeper into her lover's grasp, folding her body across him. Their lips gently parted and their tongues found each other. They kissed passionately. He cupped her ass as she continued to ride him. The fullness of that steel-hard dick inside of her was a sensory overload, and her legs started quivering.

She took a deep breath and howled out, "I'm fuckin' coming!" There was moaning, groaning, chanting, and cursing. Janet slid her body against him, his big, black dick ramming every square inch of her pussy. It was absolute pleasure.

"I'm comin'," she reiterated loudly.

Janet froze momentarily. Her G-spot had been hit numerous times. And then it happened — her pussy started flowing freely as she humped against him. She gripped the bed sheets tightly and held on for dear life, her breathing sparse and her body becoming numb. Spent, she collapsed across his chest. He had given her an earth-shattering orgasm.

"So good," she muttered to him.

The two lay motionless for a jiffy, savoring the intense feeling. Janet closed her eyes. She enjoyed the comfort of being nestled against a strong man; his arms wrapped around her, their naked black skin entwined. She could feel his heart thrashing inside his chest. He was sweaty. She was sweaty. The bedroom had heated up a few degrees.

"I need to open up a damn window." She pulled herself off of him and went to the window.

The young man gazed at her ass. For her age, she still had it going on from head to toe.

Janet lifted the window open and removed a cigarette from her dwindling pack. She lit up, took a deep pull, and exhaled. "That was nice," she said, looking out the window.

"It was," he replied.

Janet appeared detached for a moment, releasing a heavy sigh, her eyes fixed on the cars moving through the street below her bedroom window. Then her eyes shifted toward the young teenage girls lingering in front of the corner bodega with their hustler boyfriends. There was a time when she was that bitch in the hood, boosting, doing stickups, and fucking niggas for paper. She and Trina had run with the best of them, the alpha dogs in Brooklyn who got money and made a name for themselves in the streets.

The ringing phone brought her back to reality. She reached for it. "Hello."

"Janet!"

Hearing Li'l Mama's voice put a smile on Janet's face. She missed the young, sassy bitch. She knew Li'l Mama was in Miami visiting Cartier. "Li'l Mama, how's Miami?"

"I got sad news to tell you."

"What the fuck happened now?"

There was a brief pause, but Li'l Mama was never one to beat around the bush. "Trina's dead."

The unexpected solemn news made Janet gasp. "What?"

"There's no easy way to tell you this, but Prada and Fendi are dead too." Li'l Mama took a deep breath. "It's really bad down here, Janet."

"Ohmygod! What the fuck happened? Where's Cartier?"

"She ain't doin' too good."

"Who the fuck did this?" Janet shouted. "What the fuck is goin' on down there in Miami?"

"I don't know. The day I arrived, it started to jump off. We don't know who's behind everything yet. And we don't know who to turn to."

The news of Cartier's family being murdered made Janet's knees weak. She had to grab the wall to support herself.

"Another thing, Janet," Li'l Mama added, her voice cracking from having to break the news. "They kidnapped Christian, and they holdin' her for ransom."

"Oh God!" Janet hollered. "I'm on my way down there on the next plane."

"Janet, you don't have—"

"Fuck that! I'm comin'." Janet hung up.

The young man in the bed was now seated upright and staring at Janet with concern. "You okay?" he asked.

Janet spun with a hard glare aimed at him and screamed, "No, I'm not fuckin' okay. You know what? Get the fuck out! Get the fuck out my house!" She started throwing his clothes at him, and then she threw the phone and a few other solid items in his direction. "Get the fuck outta here!"

He sprung up from the bed and ducked for cover from the barrage of things being thrown his way. A lamp went flying at him like a 757, barely missing his head, smashing into the wall behind him.

"What the fuck is wrong wit' you, bitch!" he yelled.

"Leave!"

"You fuckin' crazy bitch!" He hurriedly got dressed and stormed out of Janet's apartment.

Janet slammed the door behind him. The minute she was alone, the grief swept her up like a leaflet on a windy day. She was hysterical, and her eyes were flooded with tears. She shook uncontrollably, as she leaned naked against the apartment door. It was Monya and Shanine all over again. Visions of the night she got the call that her only child, Monya and Monya's friend Shanine were both shot in the head came flooding back. Monya lingered in her coma for months, but Shanine was pronounced dead on the scene.

Janet started to tear up her apartment, turning over furniture, breaking mirrors, and kicking holes in the wall. When she was finished, she found herself sprawled out across the bathroom floor, still butt naked, her place looking like a hurricane had touched down inside.

Sing Sing State Prison

Ossining, New York

Clad in his dull gray prison attire, Head frowned as he held the phone to his ear listening to Li'l Mama. He turned his shocked expression away from the other inmates near him. They were chatting up a storm, and it was becoming hard for him to hear.

"She know who the fuck is behind this?" he snarled into the phone.

"We don't know, Head."

"This is fucked up." Head slammed his fist up against the concrete wall out of frustration. He wished his feet could touch ground in Miami to take some of the weight off Cartier. Although she had left him stranded to do his bid alone, his heart couldn't shake her.

"It is. Right now, we don't know who to trust or who to turn to. This is why I'm reaching out to you."

"Hold on a second." Head turned around and looked fiercely at the half-dozen inmates chatting and gossiping like bitches behind him. He yelled, "Y'all niggas, shut the fuck up!"

The men suddenly quieted down to a hush. Head then gave his back to the men and continued with his conversation. No one dared to defy him, knowing about his violent pedigree. Head and Nut were urban legends, and the work they put in on the streets garnered respect. He was a thorough muthafucka with connections, power, and money.

Head was hurting inside, though. His stone face tightened with anger. "Look, I'ma see what I can do for y'all. I'ma get in contact wit' one of my dudes and holla at him, so we can get that money up and have him scout fo' some info and shit."

"Thanks."

"You tell Cartier to keep her head up —" he paused, and then continued — "and that I still love and miss her."

"I will."

74

"Be careful, Li'l Mama. And I'ma get behind this shit."

The phone went dead. But Head didn't walk away yet. He stood near the phone contemplating. From what Li'l Mama had told him, it was hard to know who to pinpoint for where the hit came from. He wondered if any of his enemies were behind the murders. He knew better than to politick with any inmates outside of his crew. There were too many snitches inside, too many big-mouth muthafuckas that talked too much. He kept to himself, mostly reading and going over his case, and the only outside phone calls he made was to his lawyer and a handful of loyal members from his crew.

He needed to make another phone call. He made a collect call to a reliable soldier from his old hood. The man picked up, and Head instructed him to visit him soon.

"A'ight, I'm there, my dude," the soldier with the low, raspy voice said.

Head hung up and walked toward his cell leisurely. Behind the walls of Sing Sing, there was never a need to rush to go anywhere.

One day later, Head sat in the crowded visiting room with Scat, one of his Brooklyn soldiers. Scat was a dark black man with arms so muscular they poked out from his sides. He had a fuzzy low Afro and a scruffy beard. He was Head's go-to guy when he needed something done quickly and subtly. Scat didn't mind getting his hands dirty or taking a drive somewhere to drop off or pick up something.

Head leaned closer to Scat to keep the eavesdroppers from listening to their conversation. "I need you to make a run down to Miami for me."

Scat nodded.

"Get wit' this bitch in Queens I'ma link you to. She's holdin' a small fortune for me. I need you to take five hundred grand down to Cartier."

"You want me to make that drive alone?"

"Yeah. From what I'm told this has got to be on the low. Shit is crazy and not adding up and I'm not gonna front. I'm worried about old girl. My boo needs some protection down there, and I want you to get to the bottom of things."

Scat nodded.

"Christian is missing."

Scat leaned back in the chair, taken aback by the news. "Why?"

"I don't give a fuck about the why. I know niggas down there violated my baby, and I need that girl back wit' her moms."

Scat nodded.

"I already got it set up fo' you — money, guns. You'll be taken care of."

"A'ight."

"And Scat—" Head looked around to make sure no one was listening to their business.

Scat stared at his boss and waited for him to speak.

"I want you to kill these niggas. Do what you do best, my nigga. Show them country Miami niggas how Brooklyn gets down. Send a strong fuckin' message."

Scat smiled menacingly and nodded. "I got you, my nigga."

Both men stood up, gave each other dap, and embraced into a brotherly hug. As Scat started to make his exit from the visiting room, Head sat back down at the table and watched him depart, confident that Scat was going to get the job done.

CHAPTER 11

Cartier tossed and turned, but sleep became irrelevant when there was so much worry on her mind. Her daughter had been missing for several days now, and she was plagued by nightmares. The cell phone not ringing became a burdensome thing. Short by a half a million dollars, she had less than thirty hours to come up with it.

It was three in the morning, so things were quiet. The room was dark, the shades closed, and the 32-inch flat-panel TV mounted on the wall was off. The motel room Li'l Mama had gotten them was perfect—a Motel 6, right off the Florida Turnpike. It was a few miles south and in a secluded location. She and Li'l Mama had separate rooms directly across the hall.

Cartier lay sleepless underneath the vividly colored bedspread on the king-size bed, a .380 on the nightstand adjacent to the bed. She opened her eyes and stared at the ceiling. Frustrated about her short cash flow and the past day's proceedings, she tossed the bedspread to the floor and sat up, cursing. She then planted her feet on the carpet and stared at the accented walls.

Small comfort came to Cartier when she found out that Head was sending one of his soldiers to Miami with the remaining money for her daughter's ransom. She had expected a base hit and he was delivering a home run. Cartier knew she could always count on Head. He was a powerful man, a kingpin, and a terrific lover. Now more than ever, she regretted doing him so dirty. She wished he was free and by her side, but the state had other thoughts. Her man was in prison all because he fell in love with her.

More than anything, Cartier wanted to have her daughter home and to be nestled in Head's powerful arms. She yearned to hear him say, "It's gonna be a'ight, baby. I got this. Don't worry."

Cartier needed to find another mark. Although she anticipated the money from Head, once she paid the ransom and got Christian back, she would be dead broke. And in order to stay alive, she knew she would need to bounce. That meant getting as far away from Miami as possible. Cartier was prepared to run as far as it took to keep herself and her daughter safe. She would go deep into the land of nowhere, like Utah, or West Bumblefuck.

Cartier wanted this to be her last jux. And like with Rico, things had to go down smoothly. The Rico hit was risky but it was successful. Once the situation died down, she would unload the ki's and get ghost. With the streets definitely talking, that was going to be a feat. Things were hot, and cops were on alert. Miami was becoming like the Roaring Eighties again, with the violent murders and kidnappings.

Cartier's eyes were bloodshot. She felt like she'd aged twenty years. She reached for her pack of cigarettes and pulled one out. She lit it and took a long drag from it, savoring the nicotine surging through her body. She remained perched on her bed. The cigarettes from the pack began to dwindle as early morning moved stealthily outside the motel window, with the sun percolating through the blinds. Cartier had been up for hours.

Knocking at the door brought her out of her daze. She stood up and approached cautiously with the .380 in her hand. Looking through the peephole, she saw Li'l Mama. She unlocked the door and opened it.

Li'l Mama walked in and made an observation. "Did you get any sleep?"

"No, not really."

"You need to rest, yo. This ain't healthy for you."

"Don't tell me what to do," Cartier snapped. "Your kid ain't the one fuckin' missing!"

"Just tryin' to help out."

"I know. And I'm sorry I keep snapping, but shit is heavy."

"We gonna get the money," Li'l Mama said.

Cartier went into the bathroom to splash some water in her face and freshen up. She looked at her appearance and saw bags under her eyes. She groaned. Desperation was building inside of her. Every minute was precious, and though Head's people were supposed to be coming with the money, they needed to strike another mark in case they didn't get there in time. She was ready to go to the clubs and stick up niggas for their Rolexes, jewelry, and paper, but that wasn't going to get her the money she needed. Besides, it was too risky. Cartier stared at her reflection and said faintly, "I'ma get you back, baby."

Li'l Mama and Cartier went to meet with Quinn, hoping she had a potential victim to hit up. They picked Quinn up in front of her home and drove to the nearest diner for breakfast and a discussion. They ended up at Denny's, right off South Dixie Highway. The place wasn't crowded, and the staff was light. The girls took a corner booth near the back of the restaurant.

Cartier was on her second cup of her coffee. She truly needed the caffeine. She was pressing Quinn for another stickup. "Give me something, Quinn. Time is runnin' out."

"I got one possible mark, ay, but it's gonna be like playing Russian roulette."

"I don't give a fuck. Just say who."

Quinn looked reluctant to say who the target was. She took a sip of coffee and looked Cartier in her eyes. She saw the desperation in her friend.

"Just fuckin' say it, Quinn," Li'l Mama whispered.

"This is at least a five-to six-man job, at least . . . 'cuz this place ain't no joke. And if we fuck this up, it's gonna be a death sentence fo' all of us."

Cartier replied, "Well, it's gonna have to be a three-woman job, 'cuz we don't have time to look for anyone else, and I don't fuckin' trust no one at this fuckin' moment."

"I don't feel like dying anytime soon, Cartier," Quinn said, "so we better come wit' our fuckin' A game on this one."

Li'l Mama spat, "And you think we fuckin' do?"

Quinn ignored her. "Look, there's this meth lab, and the kicker is that it belongs to my brother."

"Hector?"

Quinn nodded.

"Oh hell no! Are you seriously gonna say you ready to set up ya own damn brother to help us out?" Li'l Mama said incredulously. "I don't believe you."

"You think I care what the fuck you believe? Do you really think you're that relevant?" Quinn was finally fed up with Li'l Mama and her accusations. "When are you gonna get it through your thick fucking head that this is about Christian!"

"It's only been about Christian for me!"

"Again, this isn't about you! I'm not helping out *you* and Christian. Or *you* and Cartier, you fucking moron."

"And why? Huh? Why are you willing to go against your own family for Cartier? Y'all ain't grow up together. We grew up together. We know each other like the back of our hands. All we are to you is some black bitches from Brooklyn," Li'l Mama said with a puckered brow.

"Fuck you, Li'l Mama! Cartier is like a sister to me."

"A sister to you? Bitch, *I'm* her fuckin' sister, and I don't trust this —"

"This isn't ya decision to make."

Cartier remained quiet, thinking about the plan.

"Cartier, I know you're not buying this. This shit has gotta be a fuckin' trap. She tryin' to set us up. We got our peoples comin' down soon, so we ain't gotta fuck wit' this bitch anymore."

"I'm really gettin' sick an' tired of you disrespecting me, Li'l Mama."

"Bitch, you feel hot then pop off!"

"Enough!" Cartier cried out.

The two looked at Cartier.

"I just wanna know when and where?" Cartier said to Quinn.

"Cartier, I know ya not seriously thinkin' about doin' this shit."

"I am."

"But —"

Cartier glared at her friend. "Li'l Mama, shut the fuck up! Do you have a better suggestion at this moment?"

"Head got his people comin' down."

"And how long will that take?"

Li'l Mama was quiet.

"Exactly!"

Quinn smirked. Li'l Mama was ready to smack that bitch, but she kept her cool and was ready to follow instructions. Whatever Cartier wanted to do, she was willing to back her one hundred percent.

"So how we gonna do this?" Cartier asked Quinn.

"Methodically."

Quinn knew if her brother ever found out she had anything to do with one of his meth labs being robbed, blood or no blood, he would literally cut the skin off her bones. It was all about respect in her gang, and with her family. Betrayal was a death sentence. And Hector would lose respect if he found out that his sister had the audacity to rob him.

But Quinn had her own hidden agenda. Helping Cartier out was also helping herself out in a big way.

The ladies ate their breakfast, but Cartier wasn't really hungry. She hadn't had an appetite since her family's murder. She nibbled on a few things and continued to glug down her hot coffee.

The three ladies exited the restaurant an hour later and went their separate ways. When Cartier was finally alone, she pulled out her throwaway cell phone to make an urgent call to New York. She parked near the overpass of the expressway underneath a rapidly graying sky. It smelled like rain.

She heard the phone ring a few times. Becoming impatient, she was about to hang up, but then she heard a woman say, "What?"

"Apple?" Cartier asked skeptically.

"Yeah. Who the fuck is this?"

"Girl, you a boss bitch in New York right now and you don't know how to answer your phone?"

"Don't play games wit' me. Speak ya business or get an earful of dial tone."

"It's Cartier."

"Oh shit! It's been so long." It felt good to Apple to hear the familiar voice of someone she had mad love and respect for. "I heard you was MIA from the game and went south."

"True. And a lot done changed."

"I see," Apple said. "Life is all about change and challenges. It separates the weak from the wolves."

Cartier became aware of the sharpness in Apple's voice. She remembered a time when the quiet, shy girl from Harlem looked up to her. Now word on the street was that Apple was now on the block and getting major paper. And she had dramatically changed, becoming a coldhearted bitch

82

and, rumor had it, a killer. Cartier had always liked Apple and her twin sister Kola. At one time, the Brooklyn native had mentored the young, wide-eyed teenager from Harlem. Cartier was the big sister that Apple had always wanted in her life.

"You a'ight?"

"Of course I am, but like you said, Cartier, a lot done changed."

"I'm at war down here."

"And I'm at war up here."

Cartier didn't want to sound insensitive to Apple's plight, but as far as she was concerned, Christian took precedence over any drama Apple was involved in. Besides, let the streets tell it, Apple was always at war. "They kidnapped my little girl. Apple. Muthafuckas took my baby!"

"What! Damn, Cartier! I'm sorry to hear 'bout that," Apple said in a sad tone. She had a pocket full of woes herself, including kid drama.

"I need a favor though," Cartier continued.

"Like what?"

"I'm goin' through it, and they holdin' my baby for ransom. I need some cash to float me and a few soldiers on loan."

"How much?"

"A hundred stacks."

"Shit, Cartier! That's pretty steep." Apple sucked her teeth. "This ain't Monopoly money you asking for."

"This is for my baby, Apple," Cartier pleaded, trying to hang on to some dignity and keep from begging. "I need my daughter back. I just can't lose her. I can't. I can't have her die because of me."

Cartier heard Apple exhale. Maybe she was contemplating giving out the loan and some of her soldiers.

Apple explained she had a crisis going on in Harlem and needed every loyal man by her side. She asked where the fuck was Cartier when bullets were whizzing past her head or when she and Kola were at war? And most importantly, she asked Cartier where was she when her daughter, Peaches, was snatched from her and sold on the black market? She told Cartier that Peaches was still out there, and yet Apple didn't call on Cartier for help. Apple read Cartier and asked where her pride was.

Cartier ignored the sermon. She could feel the shade coming from the other end and she made a promise to herself. If Apple didn't give her the support she was asking for, and if anything, anything happened to her daughter because of Apple's disrespect, then she would personally track her down and put two shots to the back of her dome. She would do the hit herself, just on GP. "Time is running out for my daughter, Apple."

Reluctantly, Apple replied, "Fifty stacks is all I can spare for now. And I'll send a man down to help you out wit' ya situation. He's on point . . . able to get any job done."

It was half what Cartier had asked for, but she was still grateful. "Thanks, Apple."

"Just get your daughter back and kill whoever's responsible for ya pain," Apple coldly advised.

"I plan to."

After the call ended, Cartier lingered in the driver's seat for a moment with the gun lying in the passenger seat. She peered at the freeway above her. The sky darkened, indicating heavy rain was about to come down on the city. And then, abruptly, the sky roared with thunder, and the heavens split open, setting free massive raindrops that cascaded off the windshield.

Rick Ross's raunchy lyrics blared throughout Mansion, the trendy Miami nightclub that resembled a mansion with its opulent chandeliers and plush interior design. The club had two levels, with high-voltage dance floors and eight bars, and was also known for its exclusive VIP areas.

Bottle service started at five large, and only the city's most elite customers were able to afford such extravagance.

Bottles of champagne were being popped all night, and the ladies, in their scanty party clothes, swarmed the dance floor, grinding and winding against their male partners. One of the exclusive VIP sections was crammed with Bones and his Miami thugs. His right-hand man, Shotta, was trying to ease the pain of losing his cousin Rico.

Bones wore loose jeans, a tight wifebeater, a belt with a large oval buckle, and a white do-rag. His scowl was intimidating, and his cold eyes manifested a seething rage building inside of him. He rested against the plush, cushioned banquette that ran along the wall of the VIP room, flanked by bitches and his crew. And in front of him was a long table cluttered with expensive bottles of tequila, vodka, champagne, Voss water, several glasses, and a bucket of ice.

Shotta was in a throwback baggy blue-and-black Adidas tracksuit that concealed his muscular frame. He wore a pair of white-on-white shell toes and dark sunglasses, his bald head gleaming like Mr. Clean's. He took a swig from the Moët bottle in his hand and lightly nudged Bones in his side, saying to him, "Playboy, we gon' find out who got Rico, an' when we do, it's gon' get fuckin' ugly."

Bones didn't respond to his friend. Rico's murder weighed heavily on his mind. It had been three days now, and the detectives didn't have any leads, though he had his own suspicions on who bodied his cousin. He wasn't looking for any handouts or favors from the cops. In his world, his henchman was the judge, jury, and executioner.

Shotta refused to leave his friend's side. He continued to sip from the bottle, his eyes on a big-booty, honey-dread ho in a short leather skirt. He leaned back in his seat, sitting like a boss with his legs spread, and the bottle between his thighs.

A moment later, one of Bones' young goons walked up with a girl in her early twenties.

"Yo, Bones, we need to talk," the youthful soldier said.

Bones wasn't in the mood to talk to anyone. "About what, muthafucka?"

"I just got some news about ya cousin, yo."

That got Bones' attention right away. Shotta sat upright also and stared at the young man togged up in sagging jeans and white tank top underneath the black leather vest and a heavy rose-gold chain around his neck.

"What the fuck about my cousin?" Bones asked.

"Shorty here says she got some info."

Bones stood up. They had his attention now.

Shotta and Bones escorted the two into the nearest bathroom. Shotta looked under the stalls to make sure they were alone, and then he stood guard by the door to prevent any unwanted company from coming in.

Bones stared at the chick. She was pretty and petite, wearing a purple dress underneath a black, cropped denim jacket, and black shoe booties. "Talk to me, shorty," he said.

The girl looked hesitant at first, feeling uneasy being the only female in the men's bathroom with three goons.

"Yo, she said she saw—"

Bones yelled, "Yo, let her talk, nigga! I wanna hear from her fuckin' mouth." Then he said coolly, "Once again, talk to me, shorty."

"I think I saw Hector's sister lingering around Rico's place the other night," she said, her voice low and childlike.

"You think, or are you sure?" Bones asked.

"It was her. She was in a truck. It was black, I think."

"The Ghost Ridas might be tryna move in on our shit," Shotta chimed. "I mean, it makes sense — take out Rico, open market."

"You think Hector would be that stupid?" Bones asked.

"I ain't ever liked or trusted that spic muthafucka anyway," Shotta said. "They sneaky. It was only a matter of time before one of them made a move."

Bones stared intensely at the young girl standing in front of him. Did she have a reason to lie or make up stories? Everyone knew the reputations of Bones and Shotta. As leaders of the Miami Gotti Boys, they were killers for hire, dealing drugs and running prostitution all over Miami.

"We can't look weak on this, Bones," Shotta said.

Bones nodded. "Y'all two get the fuck outta here."

The girl hurried out of the bathroom, followed by the hood youth.

Shotta still stood watch by the bathroom door. "It's ya call, Bones. What you wanna do?"

He barked, "I wanna fuckin' avenge my cousin's death; make every muthafucka pay for what they did."

"Then let's go," Shotta said with the screw face. "Let's make this happen."

"Fuck it. Make the call."

Shotta smiled wickedly. The Miami Gotti Boys were about to go to war with the Ghost Ridas. The two gangs had had their share of run-ins with each other over the years, fighting over territory and drug distribution, but lately things had been quiet between both violent gangs. Quiet, up until now.

Bones' stylish Impala slowly made its way into Little Havana. Moving behind the car was a dark minivan with a half-dozen armed Miami Gotti Boys, MGB. It was dusk out, and Little Havana was swamped with locals enjoying the southern heat. Some of the underground spots lining the streets were buzzing with activity and music. No one paid any attention to the slow-creeping van or the two thugs in the Impala.

The MGB members peeled the corner where a local nightspot called Pubs 'n' Shots was located. The Ghost Ridas were known to frequent the hole-in-the-wall bar nestled between Little Havana's Cuban residents and small businesses. The spot was littered with photos of gang members, past and present, thugs and drunks, and was a cash establishment only.

The Miami Gotti Boys readied themselves for an attack. Hanging around the club were close to a dozen Ghost Ridas drinking, talking shit, and gambling. Neither Hector nor any of his top lieutenants were around, but Bones was ready to send a message. He didn't give a fuck who received it.

The dark minivan with the tinted windows concealing Bones' shooters crept toward the would-be victims with UZIs and even a Heckler & Koch MP5 locked and loaded, ready for some killing. Bones and Shotta slowly drove by the club, catching a few Ghost Ridas' attention. Both camps exchanged hard stares.

Bones continued to stare his foes down as he slowly pushed his tricked-out Impala past their club.

"Fuck you lookin' at, muthafucka?" one of the Ghost Ridas shouted heatedly.

Bones smirked and tossed him the middle finger, angering a few goons. They stepped closer to the street, lifting their shirts and revealing the handguns stuffed into their jeans.

"Pussy muthafuckas!" Bones exclaimed.

As Bones unhurriedly moved through the block, coming closer to the intersection, the dark minivan came to a screeching stop in front of the club and the Ghost Ridas, and rapidly the doors slid back, revealing the MGBs, who didn't hesitate at all to open fire.

"Oh shit!" one of the Ghost Ridas shouted.

The club was quickly lit up with automatic gunfire.

Tat! Tat! Tat! Tat! Tat! Tat! Tat! Tat! Tat! Tat!

Boom! Boom! Boom! Boom!

Everyone quickly took cover as a barrage of bullets tore into everything moving, shattering glass, piercing through flesh and bones, penetrating the nightspot like it was paper-thin.

Chaos ensued. Men and women were down, crippled and bleeding from their ghastly wounds. Screams and cries of panic cut through the night air.

And then, just like that, the staccato sound of machine gun fire ended, and the minivan took off and disappeared around the next corner. The people fortunate enough to find safety and cover slowly began to pick themselves up from the ground and come out of their hiding places.

At the end of the madness, dozens were hit by gunfire, and there were four bullet-ridden bodies sprawled out on the concrete. Dead. The Ghost Ridas who had survived the onslaught stood in the middle of the street with their guns out and cursing loudly, while some tried to chase down the van, which was long gone.

"Yo, that was fuckin' Bones and his niggas," one tatted-up Ghost Rida screamed out, gripping a Glock 19 down his side, anger written all over his face.

Someone shouted, "Yo, somebody fuckin' call Hector! I can't fuckin' believe this shit!"

CHAPTER 12

Quinn, Li'l Mama, and Cartier had to map out the perfect plan to rob one of Hector's meth labs. With only three of them to pull this heist, one slipup could cost them their lives. They had to get dolled up again, show some skin and flesh and have niggas take their femininity as a sign of weakness.

The girls stood around the table with several guns displayed — 9mms, Berettas, .45s, Rugers, and a few .380s. They were ready for a small war. Each gun was carefully inspected and made ready for use. Quinn couldn't take any chances on a gun jamming, so the .22s were tossed to the side.

Li'l Mama sighed, staring at the arsenal in front of her. "I still don't trust this. It's fuckin' risky, Cartier." Li'l Mama was thorough in her own right, and had done shit in the past that most niggas wouldn't think about doing, but this caper just didn't feel right. Something in her bones said she should proceed with caution, and she knew that inner voice was usually right. If she could run out the front door without any consequence or repercussion, she would. But she knew that if she wanted to leave, she would have to kill Cartier and Quinn. Because if she left them alive, the moment Cartier got Christian back, she and/or Quinn would come for her.

Cartier wasn't in the mood to listen to her complaints. She focused on the table and picked up two chrome Berettas with black handles. "This is me, right here," she said, holding up one of the pistols and admiring it.

Quinn picked up a Ruger and the .45.

Li'l Mama picked up the black .380 ACP. She checked the clip, saw it was fully loaded and slid the gun cartridge back into position, and then cocked the hammer back.

The women looked at each other, confidence in their eyes. The deed was going down tonight.

Quinn removed a small bag and shoved her two pistols inside.

"Y'all ready?" Quinn asked.

The ladies nodded.

Quinn climbed into her truck. Li'l Mama and Cartier got into the rented Avenger. Quinn drove away first, heading toward Hector's meth lab in West Little Havana.

The ride was quiet for Cartier and Li'l Mama. Each woman had her mind on the mission as nervousness swam in her stomach.

Quinn pulled up to the quaint one-and-a-half-story, three-bedroom home on the shady residential street in the crime-ridden area. The minute her truck came to a stop in front, Hector's soldiers went on alert and gawked at the vehicle suspiciously.

Quinn got out, oozing sexiness, carrying a small bag in her hand. She smiled at the goons lingering out front in the slight chill of the night air.

"Quinn," one thug greeted. "Ay, girl, what's good?"

"Gettin' ready to hit the clubs tonight," she replied warmly.

The two goons out front eyed her but not disrespectfully. One lingering stare could get them bodied by their boss.

"Hector sent you?" the second goon asked.

"Yeah, I got a drop-off for y'all," she said.

She unzipped the bag and revealed a few chemicals the place needed to cook the meth — ammonia, a few bottles of methanol, ether, and iodine. It wasn't much in quantity, but the depot needed every little chemical available. Usually they got the chemicals in bulk, but heavy police raids and a crackdown in the purchase of certain chemicals had slowed down their supplies.

"Nice." He nodded.

She was allowed into the home without difficulty. They trusted her. She walked inside to the drug depot, and immediately she was hit with the overwhelming odor of the cloud of toxic chemicals and compounds released by the cooking process — hydrochloric acid, phosphorous, and iodine — the residue of which, over time, seeped into floors, walls, carpeting, furniture, and ventilation ducts.

For every pound of meth produced, seven to nine pounds of toxins are left behind. But it was too profitable for the gangs making the stuff to care about the environment.

The lab was in the basement, upstairs was the security and packaging. The windows were blacked out and the rooms a mess with discarded material. In the kitchen were several young butt-naked females on a tight assembly line bagging up the crystal-shaped product for street distribution. They wore surgeon's masks over their mouths, unfazed by the permanent danger that exposure to the chemicals would cause — cancer and sometimes sudden death.

In the living room were three more men, definitely armed and cautious about everything coming and going.

Quinn kept her cool. She greeted the soldiers and told them about the chemicals in the bag. She displayed it to the goons a second time, assuring the trust. But she knew something was up. Everyone was edgy. A little too edgy.

"What's goin' on, ay?" she asked.

"We got hit last night at the club," one said.

"By who?"

"Miami Gotti Boys. We at war wit' them *putos*, Quinn," he spat heatedly.

"What the fuck is wrong wit' them niggas?" she replied. "What my brother say 'bout this shit?"

"He told us to be on point and lay down anyone with two feet comin' our way!"

"That's Hector. Shoot first, ask questions never!" Quinn said jokingly, running her hands through her massive amount of jet-black hair. "Vic, let me take care of business. I'ma drop this in the room."

"A'ight."

She walked toward the hallway, but made a quick stop to the bathroom to do her business. The place was crawling with soldiers and workers. And two chemists were in the basement mixing a fortune for the Ghost Ridas.

After spending ten minutes in the bathroom, Quinn walked out and dropped the bag off into the supply room. She then came out and spent some time with the men.

"Oh, I got my girls comin' by soon," she said to Vic. "We 'bout to hit the club tonight. You know I ain't get dressed lookin' this fuckin' sexy to hang wit' y'all ugly muthafuckas."

Vic gazed at her. He was the one managing the show inside. "Nice outfit."

"Thank you." she smiled.

A few minutes later, Quinn's phone rang. It was Cartier calling. The talk was fast.

She hung up and looked at Vic.

"I got my girls comin' in," she repeated.

Vic looked unwilling. "Fo' what?"

"One of my bitches gotta use the bathroom. She ain't tryin' to piss on herself, Vic."

He scowled. "Tell her to make it quick."

"She will."

Quinn gave the girls the okay to come inside. They stepped out of the rental and strutted toward the drug depot like divas.

The two men out front were captivated by Li'l Mama and Cartier.

"Sexy," one uttered.

Li'l Mama and Cartier stepped onto the porch, but came to a standstill when Vic stepped out. "Yo, search them bitches."

"Huh?" Cartier stopped in her tracks. "Who you calling a bitch?"

"Vic, they ain't got shit on them. Look at what the fuck they wearing. Where they gonna hide anything wit' your paranoid ass!"

"I don't give a fuck. Ay, you my peoples, Quinn, not them."

Cartier and Li'l Mama stared at Quinn for advice. She shrugged.

The two goons were eager to pat them down for any weapons.

Li'l Mama and Cartier spread their legs and raised their arms, and the men quickly searched them from head to toe. Cartier felt his hands brush rapidly, yet thoroughly over any area they felt could remotely hold a weapon.

It was the same procedure for Li'l Mama.

"Y'all done?" Cartier snapped, not happy about the distrust. "I gotta pee."

"They clean, Vic."

"Happy?" Quinn said.

Vic gestured for the girls to enter. "Down the hall, first door to your left. Make it quick."

The ladies strutted into the house and quickly surveyed the area. Cartier counted five men total and the naked female workers in the kitchen. If she wanted to call the whole thing off, now was the time. This certainly wasn't going to be a cakewalk. The scheme had to be executed with accuracy.

Li'l Mama followed behind Cartier to the bathroom. No one asked questions. They walked in together, while Quinn kept the men company. In the bathroom, the girls opened the bathroom cabinet and saw the guns Quinn had left behind — two 9mms, and a .45, along with some silencers.

Cartier grabbed the two 9mms and twisted a silencer onto each barrel. Li'l Mama performed the same action with the .45.

"You ready to do this?" Cartier asked.

Li'l Mama nodded. Inwardly, she wondered if either one of them was really ready.

In the living room, Quinn strategically positioned herself near Vic, whose pistol was displayed nestled in his waistband. He was watching the bathroom.

Quinn kept ready to act, waiting for the move to happen. Two men were outside the house, the door closed; three inside, one seated, Vic by the door chatting with Quinn, and the third man seated on the arm of the sofa, his attention focused on a soccer match on television. Their guns were visible, but not in reach. Vic was the only one with his gun in his waist.

Quinn kept watching, waiting. *C'mon, c'mon, c'mon*, she said to herself. Her heart started to beat like drums against her chest. The anxiety was a motherfucker. She gazed at the three men in the room. None of them suspected anything yet. *C'mon!*

Abruptly, the bathroom door swung open, Cartier hurried out, her arms outstretched with the guns in her hands, Li'l Mama right behind her.

Vic saw, but before he could take action, Quinn snatched the pistol out of his waistband and shoved him against the wall.

Cartier opened fire first. *Poot! Poot! Poot!* She struck the man seated with three shots in his chest. He jerked violently and slumped over in the couch.

The next man watching soccer rushed to grab the Glock 17 on the coffee table, but Li'l Mama already had him in her sights and fired. Two shots tore into his side and dropped him suddenly with a *thud* and *umph!*

Vic rushed for the door trying to make a speedy escape, cursing, but he was cut short when Quinn fired his own gun into him, two rounds slamming into his chest and pushing him back into the wall.

The front door flew open, and the last two soldiers charged inside firing shots at Cartier and Li'l Mama.

Cartier immediately took one in the leg and slumped forward. "Shit!" she cried out. "I'm shot!" But it was only a graze.

Li'l Mama ducked, taking cover, and fired back.

One of the goons rushing in was quickly met with death when Quinn moved from her hiding place behind the door and put a bullet in his head.

His partner turned, and Quinn quickly took him out too, firing two shots into his head.

When the smoke cleared, the men's bodies lay scattered and contorted. The place was now full of bullet-riddled bodies, blood-spattered walls, and pools of blood. The naked bitches in the kitchen were screaming and cowering in the corner. The front exit was their only escape, since the back door had been bolted shut. This had been done early on as a precautionary measure and for their protection.

Li'l Mama inspected Cartier's wound, while Quinn went into the basement and quickly executed the two chemists. The girls made the scared, whimpering female workers lie facedown on the kitchen floor.

Quinn went to get the money. They didn't have a lot of time.

The ladies cried out in Spanish, pleading for their lives.

Cartier and Li'l Mama, their eyes cold, stood over their naked frames. "Fuck these bitches!" Cartier uttered. *Poot!* She put a bullet into the first victim's head.

Li'l Mama followed suit.

Poot! Poot! Poot! Poot!

One by one, they put to death each begging young girl lying facedown in her birthday suit. The kitchen floor was fast pooling with their blood.

When it was over, six female victims lay dead.

Quinn came rushing into the room with a black duffel bag in her hand. "Let's get the fuck outta here!"

The ladies rushed outside and into their vehicles, leaving behind the carnage for Miami-Dade to clean up and investigate. Cartier hurried into the passenger seat, and they sped off.

As Li'l Mama drove, Cartier wondered if God could forgive her for a gruesome sin like this. Can a bitch repent after this? Her mind shifted to her daughter. By any means necessary to get her little girl back, she reasoned. It didn't matter who went down and how. These people had already chosen their lives; Christian was still too young to choose hers.

At Quinn's home, Cartier was furious. Their take was disappointing — less than twenty thousand. "I don't fuckin' believe this shit!" Cartier shouted. For so many lives taken down tonight, it hardly seemed to be a fair exchange. She felt her little girl was as good as dead.

"Hector must have picked up the money earlier," Quinn speculated, looking clueless for a moment.

"What fuckin' now?" Li'l Mama asked.

❤ CHAPTER 13 ❤

The police lights outside the meth lab in West Little Havana were dizzying and blinding. It seemed like every cop in Miami had flooded the area. Yellow crime scene tape looped the investigated area, and the looky-loos, held back only by the tape and uniformed officers, were out gazing at the tragic event.

The dark Dodge came to a stop at the flood of glaring lights. Detectives Sharp and Lam climbed out of the car in their dark suits and headed toward the madness with a cool, easy stride. Everywhere they turned, there was a cop or examiner around, and the media was just arriving at the scene to film some coverage of the bloodshed.

Sharp and Lam made their way toward the house of horror, where they met with their supervisor on the porch, Lieutenant March. He stared at both men grimly and shook his head. Clad in a Miami PD police vest, his holstered Glock 19 clinging to his hip, he said, "I hope y'all two have cast-iron stomachs. It's like fuckin' Baghdad in there."

"That bad, huh?" Lam said.

"See for yourself." Lieutenant March stepped aside and allowed Sharp and Lam to tread into the nightmare.

Once inside, they were met with scattered bodies in the living room.

"Ghost Ridas, I see." Sharp was able to identify the dead men by their distinctive gang tattoos.

"Yeah, it looks that way," Lam confirmed.

"Rival gang?" March asked.

"It's likely. One of our informants stated they're at war with the Miami Gotti Boys. This all has to be connected to Rico." Detective Sharp assessed.

"Or just a robbery. Some down-on-your-luck goons looking for a quick come up." Detective Lam wasn't ruling anything out.

Next, they went into the kitchen to see the naked girls lying facedown on the floor. Sharp took in everything. He tried to absorb as much as he could. He felt his heart drop for the dead young women, who looked no older than nineteen or twenty.

"We have two more dead in the basement," March said to them. "Whoever did this are fuckin' monsters."

Lam uttered, "Fuckin' overkill."

"No argument there," Sharp replied.

Their eyes shifted everywhere in the home, and then they descended into the lower belly of the nightmare, where the detectives observed the two dead chemists, both shot point-blank in the head.

"Nice setup," Lam said, gazing at the makeshift lab.

"So, what you think?" Lieutenant March asked his prized homicide detective.

Sharp looked around the cemented basement, which had good ventilation and was well lit. The equipment the chemists used was high-end, and the mixture of supplies definitely was coming in the truckloads. He continued to roam the house before he could speculate on what had happened.

A few minutes later, he said, "I don't know. It was either an ambush, caught off guard situation. Or it could have been a push-in robbery/homicide. My best guess and from what the streets are saying, this has everything to do with MGB. Only a crew of that magnitude with a history of such violence could have pulled this off."

"So is this about turf? Payback for Rico? Or just the old fashioned stick up?" March inquired, looking perplexed.

"Could be about all three," Detective Sharp assessed. "In these drug wars, at the end of the day nothing ever really makes sense."

"You think our other home invasion is definitely linked, huh?" Lam asked.

Sharp didn't answer his partner. He stood in the center of the chaos, trying to read the crime scene. He had a knack for putting all the pieces together. He stood looking aloof for a moment. He was trained in observing the minor things, reading body language and having the dead speak to him.

"Something definitely triggered this kind of violence," Sharp repeated. "We gotta trace back to something we missed. This definitely wasn't random." He released a heavy sigh.

The coroners started to bring in multiple body bags into the house.

Detective Sharp, hit with a deep sadness, continued to scrutinize everything in the room. The murders were becoming more and more vicious, and the bodies were piling up.

"We gonna find these animals," Lam said. "And we need to find them soon."

CHAPTER 14

Janet stepped off the plane in a foul mood. Already she hated the city. She wanted to scream out, "Fuck Miami!" It had taken away her best friend Trina and two of her daughters, and Christian was kidnapped.

She made it her business to fly down and get to the bottom of things, and not a damn thing was going to stop her from coming. And she was willing to die to get Christian back. She was still a baby, still innocent and pure. She could only imagine how scared that child was and the horrors she was enduring.

Passengers poured into the busy terminal like a charge of electricity. Everyone seemed so vibrant and on cloud nine. Janet didn't have time to waste. She wheeled her carry-on luggage behind the stream of people, looking stunning in a figure-flattering black jumpsuit with a double V-cut, revealing ample cleavage and strutting in her black pumps.

The noise was giving her a headache, especially the suited white man talking in a high pitch on his phone beside her. She hissed. She felt like striking him upside is head just because of his whiney tone.

She pulled out her cell phone and dialed Cartier's number, walking briskly toward the terminal exit as she heard the phone ringing.

It was a warm, cloudless morning. She stepped outside into the sweltering city's heat, her eyebrows knitted tight in anger. "Pick up, bitch," she said to herself, her heels click-clacking against the gleamed flooring.

"Hello?"

"Cartier, I'm here. I need your location 'cuz I'm 'bout to jump into a cab and head your way."

"We're at the Motel 6 right off the Florida Turnpike, room 202."

"Motel 6?" Janet was taken aback. She figured she would be given a lavish overtop address, but then remembered that the Motel 6 was only temporary, because of the murders.

"Yeah, that's right."

"Ok, I'll be there once I get into a cab. And keep your head up, Cartier. I'm here now."

A lot had to be done, and Janet was determined to get it done. *But how?* was the question. Miami wasn't her city, but she brought with her that Brooklyn attitude and her wicked street smarts. And, together, she and Cartier were going to turn Miami upside down looking for that little girl.

She threw her luggage into the trunk and climbed into the backseat in one of several cabs idling outside the terminal. She told the driver her destination. He nodded and maneuvered his way out the airport and toward the freeway then merged onto the traffic on Dolphin Expressway.

Janet looked at the tall palm trees and sprawling developments, the towering city looming in the distance. Everything about Miami seemed to be in direct contrast with New York.

It was hot. She rolled down the window to let a cool breeze waft into the cab. "How long?" she asked the driver.

"'Bout twenty minutes, ma'am," the driver said in his thick Caribbean accent.

She sighed and leaned into the seat. She checked her phone for messages, but there were none.

She could hear the engine roaring underneath the hood. The driver had a lead foot, and she was pleased. He was swerving in and out of lanes, hitting speeds up to seventy in the sparse early-morning traffic.

The cab pulled into the curved entryway in front of the Motel 6. The place was a stone's throw from the freeway.

Janet paid the driver his fee, and he removed her bag from the trunk. She stared at the six-story structure, the motel's logo perched on top, the exterior hallway and long white railings on each floor. A cluster of palm trees decorated the front entrance. It wasn't the Ritz or Sheraton, but it seemed adequate.

She made her way inside. The lobby was quiet and quaint, no marble flooring, or extravagant structures like towering waterfalls and stoned statues. There was complimentary fresh brewed coffee in the lobby.

Janet strolled past the clerk behind a stretched reception desk cluttered with pamphlets and various things. The clerk raised her head from the computer screen, noticed the luggage she was wheeling, and didn't attempt to say anything or ask questions. She went on with her business.

Janet pushed for the elevator and waited. It didn't take long. She stepped inside and pushed for the second floor. It was a short lift to the second floor. She stepped out and searched for room 202. It was the last door down the exterior hallway. To her right were the teal room doors, and to her left, a two-story drop over the railing, and beyond that, a bland and boring part of Miami. There was an off-brand gas station next door, a few local businesses across the street, and farther down, the Southland Mall. And across the highway, sprawling middle-class homes that stretched for miles.

She knocked hard.

The door to the room opened, and Janet stood face to face with Cartier. She already saw the wear and tear happening with her friend. It looked like Cartier had lost weight. Her hair was in disarray. She was clothed in booty shorts, a T-shirt, and tube socks, and her eyes were red.

"You look like shit," Janet said.

Before she could walk inside, Cartier collapsed into her arms and started to cry.

Janet clutched her tight and embraced her lovingly. "I'm here, baby. I'm here to help out wit' this," she said.

"I'm lost, Janet. I don't know what to fuckin' do any more. They got my baby," Cartier wailed. "They got my baby."

The ladies went inside the room. Li'l Mama was seated on the bed, pulling on a blunt. She greeted Janet with a head nod. It was a painful moment for everyone.

Janet continued to hold Cartier in her arms, consoling her friend. She surveyed the room, four pistols on the wooden, round table along with scattered junk food. The shades were closed, and the room reeked of weed. The television was on, showing the news, but it was on mute.

Ironically, the screen was displaying the women's most recent work — the thirteen bodies found in a meth lab. Neither girl paid the news any attention; they wanted to forget about the other night.

Janet took a seat on the bed. She had to be the strong one. Even though the news hit her hard, reminding her of the loss of her own child Monya two years earlier, she was determined not to appear crushed.

Cartier finally took a breather from her own pain just to ask about Jason Jr.

"He's fine. He's in sleep-away camp for three weeks. The bus picked the kids up two days ago."

"Why didn't you mention it to me?" Cartier asked.

"I mentioned it to Trina. Ain't no need for me to be repeatin' shit."

Cartier nodded, suddenly looking off toward the window at the mention of her slain mother.

Li'l Mama began filling Janet with information about their past escapades — the murders and stickups.

Janet uttered, "Y'all bitches did what you had to do. Trina and I would have done the same thing in the same situation. Don't sweat it."

Today was the day that Cartier expected a phone call from the kidnappers. Was her daughter still alive? Minutes felt like years for her, but she yearned for that phone to ring.

Li'l Mama continued to tell Janet about the high ransom Christian's kidnappers were asking for, and even mentioned Quinn.

Janet asked with a raised brow, "Who's Quinn?"

"She's cool peoples," Cartier said, immediately.

"And you trust this bitch?"

"Exactly!" Li'l Mama stated.

"I ain't got any reason to doubt her right now. She's been on point since we met."

"And how long have you known this bitch?" Janet felt as if she had to be overprotective.

"A few months."

Janet sucked her teeth. "Where she at now?"

"It was her brother's spot we hit last night. So she wit' her people, makin' sure everything cool and that we're not suspected."

"A'ight, look, first, a bitch is hungry. Li'l Mama, run and get us somethin' to eat."

Li'l Mama nodded.

"And then we just gotta wait for the phone call to happen," Janet said. "We gonna get this shit wrapped up. These muthafuckas don't know who they fucking wit'."

Hours went by, and nothing. It was reaching noon, and not a single phone call came through. Cartier began to worry. She needed to know something. The lack of communication from her daughter's kidnappers was killing her inside. It felt like her intestines were tied into one big knot and someone was pulling from both ends.

Li'l Mama was waiting on word from Head. The muscle he sent should have already arrived into Miami, but so far, there was no show and no word. She didn't want to worry. Miami was a long drive from New York. She took a sip of Vitamin Water and nibbled at her breakfast.

Quinn called Cartier's phone, informing her that some FedEx package had come for her. She'd signed for it and wanted to drop it by the motel. Curiosity got the best of both girls, as Quinn was on her way to drop it off.

"Why aren't they fuckin' calling?"

Cartier stared at the time. It was ten minutes after one. She was very edgy. She barely broke half a million for the ransom. Failure plagued her mind and heart. Seated at the edge of the bed with cell phone in hand, she gazed at Janet, maybe looking for answers or some advice.

"They gonna call," Janet said.

Knocking at the door made them jumpy.

Li'l Mama stood up, picked up the pistol from the table, and proceeded to the door carefully. She cocked it back and looked through the peephole.

"Quinn." Li'l Mama turned the locks and let her inside.

Quinn walked into the room holding the small FedEx package. "Any word?" she asked.

Cartier shook her head.

Quinn placed the package in her lap.

"What is this?" Cartier asked.

"Don't know. It came this morning, no return address."

As Cartier was about to open the package, the cell phone rang. She snatched it up and answered frantically. "Yeah!" It felt like rocks were in her throat

"I told you, don't fuck with us!" the distorted voice hissed sharply.

"W-what? What did I do?"

"You violated specific orders — I told you not to bring in any outside goons or your daughter is dead."

"But I-I didn't. I swear, I didn't," she cried out. "Please don't hurt her."

"Don't fuckin' lie to us!"

"Oh God!"

"Have you received our package?"

Cartier stared at the small box in her lap. She was baffled. "I have it wit' me."

"Open our gift then."

Cartier at once tore open the package and then looked aghast at the content inside. She screamed and tossed the box off her lap onto the bed, leaping from where she sat.

Li'l Mama and everyone else rushed over to see what was inside. They all became horror-struck at the human hands inside.

Cartier started crying, fearing the hands belonged to her daughter. But at second glance, it was clear they belonged to someone older — an adult male.

"You fuckin' bastard!" she shouted into the phone.

"Next time, I'll send you your daughter's hands. They're soft and precious, you know. I'll cut this little bitch's shit off from the wrist down," the voice said in a malicious tone.

"I swear to God," Cartier screamed, "if you fuckin' touch one hair on her head, I will hunt you down and kill you!"

"You're in no position to make threats. I'm done fuckin' around with you. If your jailbird lover interferes again, we will kill her. If he even attempts to find out about us, not only will I butcher this little bitch nice and slow, I will come back for you and do the same. Got me, bitch?"

"Please, just don't hurt her. Let me talk to her."

"You didn't answer the fuckin' question."

"Yes, I understand." The tears were rivers coming down Cartier's face. She had never felt so helpless or defenseless. "Can I talk to her?"

"Do you have our money?"

Cartier hesitated. "I only have half of it."

"That's not enough!" he exclaimed.

"I can get the rest. I just need more time. I can get it."

"Time? You ran out of time."

"No!" Cartier said frantically. "Please, I have five hundred thousand. I can get you the rest."

"We want our money. But I'll do you a favor. Make the drop today, and that will give your daughter one more week."

"I want to hear from my daughter first. I want proof of life."

"Proof of life." He chuckled. It was cold and sinister.

The phone went silent, and then Cartier heard, "Mommy."

"Baby, I'm here. Talk to me," Cartier cried out.

"Mommy, I'm scared. I'm scared, Mommy." Christian's voice was shaky and faint.

"Christian, don't be scared. Where are you?"

"There's your proof of life. We will text you the location and time. Don't fuck with us!" The caller hung up.

Cartier was hysterical. She broke down, falling to her knees, her eyes flooded with tears, and her face washed with unbelievable grief. Knowing her baby was still alive stirred up some hope inside of her.

"What happened? What they say?" Li'l Mama asked.

"What's goin' on wit' the drop?" Quinn asked.

Cartier was planted on her knees, in surrender. She choked up in tears and couldn't answer any questions right away. Hearing her daughter's voice had made things more painful.

"Talk to us, Cartier," Janet said. "What did they want?"

"She's alive. She-she-she —" Cartier was finding it hard to speak.

Janet sat on the floor with Cartier and pulled the grieving mother into her arms. "Fight this, Cartier. Don't break down on us now. Christian needs you to remain strong. We gonna find her. We gonna get her back, at any cost," she said with conviction. "Fight this and become angry."

Cartier dried her tears. Janet was right. It was good to hear Christian's voice, but the way she sounded dropped Cartier's heart into the pit of her stomach.

Li'l Mama's phone rang. She answered, stepping near the window to speak. "Who this?"

"You have a collect call from Head. If you wish to accept, please press one. If —"

Li'l Mama accepted the call right away.

Head's thunderous voice boomed through the receiver, "Is Cartier a'ight?"

Li'l Mama was caught off guard by his worried tone. "Head, what up?"

"Where's Cartier? Let me talk to her."

"Hold on." Li'l Mama walked over to Cartier and handed her the phone. "It's Head."

At first, Cartier seemed reluctant to take the call. But she needed answers and assurance. The soldier coming down from New York was MIA, and now it seemed as if the kidnappers knew her every move. They were watching and probably listening. She had to be careful. These weren't the run-of-the-mill muthafuckas from the block.

Cartier took the phone from Li'l Mama. "What's goin' on, Head?"

"Ma, shit got thick. I got word that they bodied my li'l man. He didn't make it to you did he?"

"No, Head." Cartier felt despair. "He didn't make it here, I didn't get the money, and now Christian's life is in danger . . . all because of you!"

"Because of me?" Head was incredulous. He wanted to scream at her, but he was older and wiser than the average. He knew she was at her wit's end, under tremendous pressure, and wasn't in her right mind. So, he allowed her to vent. "Na, ma, you don't mean that. Listen, let me do this again but the right way. I'll send a crew of thoroughbreds down there to get at those niggas. And I'll also have them personally bring you another half mil."

Cartier shook her head violently and screamed, "No! That is too dangerous. What I need to know is who the fuck did you speak to about this shit? Who?"

"The only person I spoke wit' is dead, Cartier. And everything I did was for you."

Cartier heard the sincerity in his voice. This was Head. The man who loved her. "How did they know then? How on earth could they have known?"

"Someone in your camp is a fuckin' snitch, and 'cuz of that, Scat is dead."

Cartier realized Head was right. The noose had tightened and it was becoming harder to breathe. The phone call went dead, and Cartier was left with a million and one concerns and problems.

Cartier glared at Li'l Mama. "Bitch, who the fuck did you tell about Scat and the money?"

Li'l Mama looked dumbfounded. "What?"

Cartier pointed her index finger in Li'l Mama's face. "Who the fuck did you tell about Scat comin' down wit' the money?"

"I didn't tell a damn soul. The only person who knew about Scat driving down was you, me, Janet, Head, and whoever Scat told—if he was stupid enough to tell anyone."

Just then, Cartier received a text from the kidnappers with the location where they wanted her to drop the money off. Cartier stared at the text for the moment. She knew the area. A tense feeling swept over her. This was it. This money would give her daughter an extra week, but after the drop, then what?

❦ CHAPTER 15 ❦

Hector sat scowling and seething in the backseat of the Hummer H2 with dark tint. He hissed, "Fuckin' Bones . . . we gon' skin this fuckin' *puto* to bones." In his grip was a fully loaded sawed-off shotgun.

Tumble was driving the truck, and riding shotgun was another killer, Pico. The men wanted bloodshed.

The bloody invasion of one of Hector's meth labs was a hard blow. The horrendous crime had made front-page news. Word on the streets was, the Miami Gotti Boys were at war with the Ghost Ridas.

Within twenty-four hours, the Ghost Ridas had been hit hard, first at the club, and then their meth lab. Unbeknownst to them, other evils had their hand in their pocket, but Hector was too upset to think rationally. His men wanted payback, and so did he.

Rime, Dotter, Shawn, Freddy, and Vic were all killed in the meth lab, along with his two first-rate chemists and six homegirls. Then some men were gunned down at the Pubs 'n' Shots. Oh, some people had to die.

"We gon' find these *putos*, Hector. We gon' show who not to fuck with," Tumble said gruffly.

Hector looked intently out the window and remained quiet as he took a drag from his cigarette.

The monstrous silvery vehicle sat perched on 26-inch chrome rims that gleamed like rolling mirrors as it moved through Liberty City. People lingering on the street stared at the flashy vehicle, which definitely stood out in the hood. It looked like a rolling tank. Street-smart individuals knew something was up.

Tumble drove into Little Haiti, the traditional center for Haitian immigrants and francophone culture in the city. Adjacent to Liberty City, it was a ruthless area with crime and violent gangs. Liberty City and Little Haiti, two hoods that were known hangouts for the MGBs, were cluttered with abandoned cars in unkempt front yards, alleyways, and vacant lots. There was trash-covered intersections, and low-income housing. But these men weren't intimidated. They had a score to settle and an image to uphold. They drove around with lethal payback on their agenda.

The night was cool and cloudless, multiple stars painted across the sky. The Hummer slowly turned onto a residential street cluttered with aged cars and poorly maintained homes. There was a gathering at the end of the street, where Haitians were partying, and a few Miami Gotti Boys were in attendance. The music could be heard blaring a block away, and the front of the house crammed with gang members, mostly Miami Gotti Boys, and a few Haitians all mixed in with innocent civilians.

"Hector, there go a few right there," Tumble said. "One-eighty-seven on these *putos,* ay."

Hector nodded. He cocked back the sawed-off shotgun and instructed his peoples to proceed cautiously. They were ready to put a violent and abrupt end to the joyous party. There was no clue that Bones or any of his close henchmen were at the party, but a loud and serious statement was about to be sent out.

The Hummer moved through the block slowly, its headlights off and the windows down. Hector and the front passenger were perched out of the window with their weapons in hand, the sawed-off in Hector's hands, and Pico gripping an UZI.

Pico growled, "Lay 'em down."

Out front, three Miami Gotti Boys were leaned against a dark Benz, passing around a burning blunt and sipping on Henny. The block was in darkness; towering trees, thick shrubberies, and broken street lamps gave the approaching Hummer H2 the stealth it needed.

There were about two dozen folks lingering outside in the tattered front yard. The girls were laughing and flirting, and the young men were dancing, some trying to pick up phone numbers.

Two more Miami Gotti Boys, flaunting their tattoos and gang colors, black and green, exited the backyard to join their cohorts on the street near the Benz. And then a few scantily clad females joined the group to share in the weed and alcohol.

As the Hummer moved close, Hector had his sights set on the Benz surrounded by his foes. He had a firm grip on the shotgun and was ready to cut loose.

Tumble sped up. He was wishing he could kill a nigga too, but he was the driver tonight.

One of the Gotti Boys quickly noticed that something wasn't right. He nervously tapped his partner next to him to point out the truck approaching with no headlights.

Boom! Boom!

The shotgun exploded in Hector's arms, sending one gang member flying across the hood of the Benz with a shotgun blast to his chest. And Pico's UZI tore into a few goons, ripping through flesh, spattering blood, and violently twisting the men to death.

Panic ensued as people in the front yard started to scatter for cover. Screaming was heard everywhere. A few Miami Gotti Boys tried to return gunfire, but the heavy barrage of bullets coming from the Hummer sent them retreating for their own lives.

Tumble pushed his foot against the accelerator, and the Hummer went screeching off down the block and into the night. The three men were satisfied with the carnage they left behind.

When the smoke cleared, four men lay dead and several others wounded, including three females and a young girl. The surviving Miami Gotti Boys stood among the chaos, fuming. They'd caught the make of the truck, but not the plate number. But it didn't take Einstein to know it was the Ghost Ridas, with Hector leading the charge.

Detective Sharp reentered the crime scene on Brickell Avenue. He removed the crime scene tape from the door and looked around. The high-rise condo still smelled of death. The bodies had been taken out, but the horrors of what had happened inside still lingered. He was alone as he painstakingly looked around, wearing his latex gloves and watching his every step. His gut feeling was telling him to go back and search for something. He knew he had missed something that day.

He went through the living room first, focusing his attention on every minute detail. It was hard to see such a lavish and affluent place as the scene of such ghastly murders, but in his line of work, he had seen it all.

Sharp stepped out onto the terrace, which was lit up by the full moon. He could feel the gentle breeze coming off the waters. He gazed out at the scenery. The aura of the lights seemed to bring calm over him, but it was short-lived. He had murders to solve and a city to protect, if you could call it that. He lingered for a moment, his mind recollecting the past events.

"Fuckin' Miami," he said softly.

He took a deep breath and stepped back into the apartment, his mind transitioning into that of an astute crime-scene investigator again. He walked over to where they'd found the young sisters murdered and fixed his eyes where the bodies once lay. He stood for a moment, thinking.

His cell phone buzzed in his inner jacket pocket. He reached inside and answered. "Talk to me."

"We have another one," Detective Lam said.

Sharp sighed heavily. "Where?"

"Little Haiti — four dead, several shot. It looks like the Ghost Ridas decided to give the Miami Gotti Boys some payback."

"We gonna have a serious problem, Lam."

"Where are you now?"

"At the apartment on Brickell Avenue."

"Why?"

"We missed something here. I can feel it. I'm just retracing our steps."

"Hurry that up, and when you're done there, meet us at Middle East. It's fuckin' war on terror out here," Lam joked.

Sharp hung up, not amused by his partner's sense of humor.

He continued going through the apartment, his soft eyes going everywhere. He went into the bedroom, the kitchen, and the girls' room. What was the reason for the home invasion? Why the slaughter on a house full of women? Detective Sharp wanted to know if there was a connection between the war brewing between the Ghost Ridas and Miami Gotti Boys. Sharp wanted to know who the man of the house was. Perhaps there was a baby daddy, brother, someone either down with MGB or Ghost Ridas that had a mark on his head.

Sharp looked around the apartment until he found the family's photo album. He saw the regular run-of-the-mill stuff; better times. A light-skinned man with expensive jewelry and cars; some pictures had this same man holding guns and wads of cash. He was most certainly a dope boy. He saw Cartier in various poses with different women, undoubtedly her friends.

Sharp was ready to interview Cartier. He felt in his heart that she had information, and he was going to make it his business to squeeze the truth out of her, her friends, and anyone involved.

CHAPTER 16

The drop had to be made alone. Cartier didn't want to disobey the kidnapper's instructions and risk her daughter's life. Hearing Christian's voice had brought some light back into her and made her determined to get the job done. She had one additional week to come up with another half a million, and she wasn't going to fail this time.

Late that afternoon on a warm day with blue skies all around, she drove the rented Dodge Avenger toward Miami Airport with the half a million in a duffel bag on the front seat. She made sure to keep the money close. She navigated through airport traffic and pulled into the terminal garage. The airport was flooded with traffic, people, and security.

She found a parking spot and stepped out of the car in her blue jeans, white Nike, and fitted T-shirt that highlighted her breasts; her hair in one long braid. She wanted to dress down, nothing gaudy. She removed the duffel bag from the passenger seat. Now it was time to proceed with the kidnappers' demands. They had to be watching.

She clutched her cell phone and the duffel bag like it was her lifeline. She arrived at the garage at six. The garage was poorly lit and inundated with cars, so she'd chosen to park on the third level. She walked toward the terminal, where the arrival passengers were making their way into the terminal, which was so full of movement.

Cartier stood in the center of it all, aghast at such confusion and thinking, *How clever.* The kidnappers had ordered her by text to make the drop-off at a certain arrival terminal, but it was a zoo inside. She assumed they wanted this type of confusion. If she was being followed, then it was hard to spot her among the crowd inside. She stood there looking dumbfounded, awaiting further instructions.

Soon, the text came into her phone:

GO INTO THE WOMEN'S BATHROOM AND ENTER THE LAST STALL. WAIT FIVE MINUTES, AND WALK OUT. LEAVE THE MONEY IN THE STALL.

Cartier took a deep breath. That was simple enough. The women's bathroom was to her right, near the public exit. She proceeded that way. When she stepped into the bathroom, there was only one occupant, a well-dressed, chocolate-complexioned woman with auburn dreads who stood by the mirror checking her makeup.

She stopped abruptly, gazing at the woman by the mirror. *Is this the bitch that helped take my daughter and slaughtered my family? Is she here for the money?*

The woman noticed Cartier staring. She stopped what she was doing and returned the stare. "Can I help you with something?"

"No, I'm okay."

The lady rolled her eyes and caught an attitude.

Who is she? Cartier was ready to confront this bitch. Maybe she wasn't in on the kidnapping and was just another occupant in the bathroom. She had no way of knowing.

She walked past the woman and, as instructed, went into the last stall, which happened to be empty. She closed the door and asked herself, *Now what?*

Five minutes later, she stepped out the stall, leaving the duffel bag on the lid of the toilet. By that time, the other woman was gone from the bathroom. Exiting the ladies' bathroom, uneasiness overcame Cartier. Leaving a half a million dollars in a bathroom stall was foolish, but her hands were tied.

She was then instructed to exit the terminal and walk back to her car, which she did. Cartier didn't even bother to turn around and see who was going in or leaving the bathroom, for fear that looking back would have been a violation and would have angered the kidnappers.

Coolly, she walked back to the garage and climbed into her car. Taking a deep breath, trying to stay calm, she lingered behind the wheel and waited. Her hands shook a tad, and her eyes shifted everywhere. Everyone was a potential threat — anyone in the area was a foe to her, no matter how they looked or who they were — cop, passenger, airline employee, a couple.

Her cell phone rang loudly.

Cartier jumped and answered quickly. "Hello?"

"You did good, but plans have changed," the distorted voice said.

"What you mean?"

"You fucked with us, so now the ransom is double — another million owed."

Cartier screamed, "Are you fuckin' crazy!"

"Don't disrespect me."

"Where I'm gonna get another million? We agreed another five hundred thousand, that's the promise," Cartier cried out, the tears building in her eyes.

"Interest owed for not having the full amount. And punitive damages."

Cartier wanted to reach through the phone and break his fucking neck. She was ready to punch out the windshield. "Where's my little girl? I wanna talk to her," she pleaded.

Christian's voice surged through the phone. "Mommy, I'm scared."

"Baby, what are they doin' to you? Are they feeding you?" Cartier cried out. Her eyes were flooded with tears. The anguish was killing her slowly inside.

"Help me, Mommy."

"I'm gonna get you back, baby. I promise that. I'm gonna get you back."

"We want our million by next week, or the only thing you'll have of your daughter is memories."

Cartier went into a convulsion, punching the steering wheel, screaming loudly, and banging her fist against the window. She felt like shit. They were torturing her.

Then she slumped into the seat, spent. The tears wouldn't stop, and the pain felt everlasting.

For the first time since this saga began, she thought, if only for a fleeting moment, to involve the feds.

Cartier, Janet, Quinn, and Li'l Mama sat around in the motel room contemplating their next score.

"I shoulda went wit' you, Cartier," Li'l Mama said.

"And do what, besides get my daughter killed? You know I was instructed to go alone. And they watching us."

Li'l Mama said, "That's a half a million gone, and what now? More instructions."

"I'll tell you what now — We get busy lookin' for our next target. We got one week to get this money. And if more blood gotta spill, then so fuckin' be it. But as for now, my daughter's well-being and her coming home is my first fuckin' priority."

Li'l Mama sucked her teeth.

"What the fuck you suckin' your teeth for, Li'l Mama?" Cartier shouted. "This is my daughter they fuckin' have, not yours!"

"I know that."

"You don't know shit, bitch! You actin' scared all of a sudden. You wanna back out now and fuck me over, then fuckin' say so."

"I didn't say that."

"Then what you saying?"

"There's gotta be another plan to this shit, Cartier. We doin' what we can, busting our ass."

"And? What? You wanna involve the police or somethin'?"

Li'l Mama stood quiet, but her look told it all.

Cartier right away read what she was thinking. "Bitch, you out ya gotdamn mind?"

"I didn't say all that."

"Then what the fuck are you saying?"

"Look, they playin' fuckin' games wit' you, Cartier. Wit' us. Can't you see it? This is bigger than us now."

Cartier glared at her friend and screamed, "No feds, no fuckin' police. Fuck them! I'ma get Christian back, with or without you."

Li'l Mama sighed. She had vowed to help at any cost, but Cartier was thinking unreasonably. A half a million dollars was gone, and now they wanted another million from her. Li'l Mama knew there was something wrong with the entire picture.

"You need to get yourself together and fuckin' think, Cartier," Li'l Mama exclaimed. "They're fuckin' playin' us. We don't have this under control. We out there slaughtering niggas just to come up wit' this fuckin' ransom. How long you think it's gonna last until we get bodied out there ourselves?"

Cartier shouted, "If you wanna be a scared fuckin' bitch all of a sudden, then that's you! But I'ma come up wit' the money!"

Li'l Mama shook her head. It was like trying to bring down a cement wall with only her fists. Cartier was just too headstrong.

"You either gonna stay wit' me or not. But I'ma get her back, and they gonna fuckin' pay for what they did to us."

"And who's *they*? We don't even have a fuckin' name, Cartier. Not even a fuckin' face to put to the muthafucka calling. Who the fuck we fighting? They smart enough to keep themselves invisible, but they steady watchin' us, right? We need fuckin' help."

Cartier felt that involving any type of law enforcement would certainly get Christian killed. She felt it was easier to come up with the million than involve the feds. It was against the code in her world to include cops, especially the feds. *Is Li'l Mama crazy?* And the feds would surely fuck things up and start to investigate her, Li'l Mama, Janet, and everyone else in their circle.

"I got help, bitch! You and Quinn. What the fuck you think you good for?"

"Cartier, I'm not gonna keep being disrespected after everything I've done for you. So since you got shit on lock, I will gracefully bow out of this one. You and Quinn can go with guns blazin' for all I care."

This wasn't what Cartier wanted to hear. She took the base out of her voice. "What does that mean?"

"It means, I ain't down wit' the next robbery."

Cartier felt like she'd been punched in her gut. Li'l Mama had temporarily snatched her breath. If Cartier lived a hundred years she felt she could never come to terms with Li'l Mama kicking her when she was down. Cartier felt betrayed and enraged beyond measure. She wanted to tear her into tiny little pieces and feed her to wild animals. In a low, ominous tone, she stated, "If you want out, then you're out."

"Y'all two bitches need to fuckin' chill," Janet chimed. "Look at y'all.

We family, and y'all ready to tear into each other like strangers. Y'all go back since how long? Huh?"

Cartier and Li'l Mama glared at each other.

Janet added. "Look, we either work together on this, or we don't. And if we don't, then that little girl is as good as dead. And we're not involving the feds or anybody, Li'l Mama. You know better than that. We don't bring outsiders to solve our fuckin' problems."

"What's the plan then?" Li'l Mama asked.

Cartier was looking forward to Janet's wisdom. She was street, all day, every day.

"Me and your mother, Cartier, back in the days, we had heart. And I'm not sayin' you don't have heart; you do. I watched you grow up and used to change your damn diapers, so I know what kind of blood runs through you. You from the Stuy, you and Li'l Mama, and it's always Bed-Stuy, do or die, all day, every day. You hear me? You do what you gotta do in this game, but don't fight your own peoples."

Cartier nodded. "So what now?" she asked.

"Y'all pick and choose who to go after," Janet said, "but it's gotta be big and worth the risk. Attaining a million in one week is nothin' to sneeze at."

"It ain't gon' be easy at this moment," Quinn said. "After our last two hits, wit' the bodies we dropped, these drug crews out there are becoming wiser an' muscling up double time at their stash houses. They don't trust anyone. We done started some shit. It's war out there."

It was the one thing Li'l Mama and Quinn agreed on.

Janet asked them, "So, who's out there right now sittin' on a mountain of cash?"

The room was quiet for a moment. The girls were thinking.

Cartier then stared at Quinn. "Hector."

"Are you crazy?" Quinn yelled.

"Yes, I am. I don't give a fuck!"

"That's suicide, Cartier," Li'l Mama said. "A death check waiting to be cashed in."

"He's the only one we know fo' sure that has money like that. And he needs to be got."

"Hector will kill us all," Quinn said.

"And my daughter is as good as dead if I don't pull this off."

Quinn huffed.

Janet said, "Like I told y'all bitches . . . y'all do what ya gotta do, but get that li'l girl back."

"Why not just ask him for the money?" Li'l Mama reasoned. "He's Quinn's brother, is checking for Cartier, and also said he would help out."

Quinn laughed hysterically. "He might be kinda sweet over Cartier but he ain't never tasted her pussy. And although he's my brother, I can barely get a dollar out of him. You see, that's why I gotta take mines. When my brother said he would help out, he meant do the most easiest thing that comes natural to him. Kill people."

Cartier walked closer to Quinn, exasperated. The desperation showing in her eyes said she wasn't going to take no for an answer. "Quinn, I need to do this. And I know he's your brother, but wit' your blessing or not, it's goin' down."

They locked eyes, each one trying to read the other's expression.

Quinn was drowning in her guilt. The blood on her hands was thick. A war between two gangs was raging out of control; so far almost a dozen Ghost Ridas were murdered. And now this, it was suicide for sure.

Cartier knew she was asking a lot from her friend.

Finally, Quinn gave in. She said to Cartier, "I'll help strategize everything, but I'm out on this one. I can't go against blood like that."

"Whatever."

Li'l Mama snorted. How easy it was for Quinn to be out of this robbery, and Cartier didn't dare have any objections. Li'l Mama was salty at how much Cartier was showing allegiance to this new chick. She wanted to yell so many things, mainly about how she didn't trust Quinn, but she didn't. She finally remained mute. There wasn't anything to say that she hadn't said.

"The best I can do for you is to make sure he isn't around when it happens. I don't want him hurt at all. And the place you thinkin' 'bout robbin', Cartier, I warn you now, Hector got it locked down tighter than Fort Knox."

The fire in Cartier's eyes showed her mind was cemented. "I'll go through hell for my daughter."

"I know you will."

Cartier turned to Li'l Mama, who was quiet, looking reluctant. "You down wit' me, Li'l Mama?"

"This is suicide, Cartier — you know it, and Quinn definitely knows it. What good are you gonna be to ya daughter if we die doin' this?"

"You backin' out on me, bitch?"

"First off, I ain't no fuckin' bitch; my blood runs cold like yours. I just want you to think for once, have common sense in ya head. We got away twice. We pushin' it. I have a bad feeling 'bout this."

Cartier looked at Li'l Mama and had serious doubt. Once again, suspicion of Li'l Mama started to swell inside of her. Why was she continually fighting her, tooth and nail, on everything since she stepped foot into Miami?

"It's either yes or no."

"I'll do it." Li'l Mama felt like she didn't have a choice. "Quinn is out, so who's gonna be the third person?"

"I have someone."

"Really? Who?"

"Don't worry about him," Cartier spat.

Hearing *him* had everyone speculating.

Li'l Mama asked, "*Him? Him,* who the fuck is *him?*"

Unbeknownst to Li'l Mama and everyone else in the room, Apple had come through on her word and sent a soldier down for muscle, along with fifty thousand dollars, and he was staying in a hotel not too far from them.

"Don't worry about it. I always got a few tricks up my sleeve," Cartier gloated.

"I see that."

"You know what, Li'l Mama? You actin' fuckin' suspect right now."

"You the one actin' fuckin' crazy. I got ya back and always had ya back for a long time, Cartier. You know this."

"I don't know shit anymore. Anybody could be lying to me at this moment."

"Fuck you! I'm goin' all out fo' you down here in Miami, bodying' muthafuckas fo' you, and you step to me like I'm a lying bitch or hidin' somethin' from you. Shit, we goin' through all this, and Christian might be already dead!"

"What did you just say?" Cartier went berserk. She lunged for Li'l Mama and started to strike her repeatedly.

Li'l Mama was hit so hard with a right to her face and stumbled backwards, becoming a little bit disoriented, and then was slammed into the wall, and the girls tussled.

Cartier was incredibly strong and showered her with a few vicious blows. "You bitch!" she screamed.

"Get the fuck off me! Get off me!" Li'l Mama screamed.

Janet and Quinn rushed over.

Janet grabbed Cartier and pulled her off Li'l Mama. "What the fuck is y'all problem?" Janet was screaming too. "What I just say to y'all?"

"Fuck her, Janet!"

"Bitch, how fuckin' dare you put ya fuckin' hands on me, Cartier!" Li'l Mama shouted. "I've been there for you from day one, and you fuckin' do me like this?"

Quinn and Janet stood between them as they scowled at each other. Li'l Mama had a bloody lip.

Janet told them, "This bickering between y'all two is not helping us or Christian at all."

"I'll be in the fuckin' lobby, alone," Cartier said to everyone. She snatched up her things and made a quick exit from the room.

As Cartier marched down the hallway, it suddenly dawned on her. The soldier that Apple had sent down made it into Miami in one piece — money and all, but Scat didn't. Li'l Mama knew about Scat, but she didn't know about Mills. Cartier didn't tell a soul that she'd contacted Apple.

Cartier knew she'd pinpointed the betrayal. It had to be Li'l Mama, whose sudden resistance was clear as day. Li'l Mama had to be in on everything.

CHAPTER 17

Despite everything going on, Cartier had to bury her family. And there was no way she was going to bury her mother and sisters in Miami. She had made arrangements to fly the bodies back to New York, and have them shipped to a funeral home in Brooklyn, where they would be readied for burial. She wanted to leave the city, but she wasn't going anywhere until she had Christian with her.

Janet agreed to fly back with the bodies. Cartier trusted her to handle everything up north. Cartier stood teary-eyed with Li'l Mama and Quinn above the cargo area to watch the caskets loaded into the plane from the tarmac. The ground crew loaded her mother's casket first, which, like her sisters' caskets, was concealed in a long wooden crate for shipment. Cartier had taken care of the costly shipping fees, taking the money out of the ransom. She and Janet had to deal with the removal of the deceased, embalming, filing of documents, and a combination shipping unit and delivery to the departure airport. And she had the services of a funeral home at the destination airport to handle the collection of the deceased. It was tedious business, but for her family's final moment, it had to be done.

Li'l Mama stood close to her friend, with whom she had reconciled somewhat. Li'l Mama shed her own tears as she watched the bodies being loaded onto an American Airlines flight. The women's hearts were heavy with grief, each one silent. They'd lost a lot, and it was a scary time for everyone.

Cartier watched Janet board the plane behind a line of other passengers. There were no smiles, no goodbyes, or waves. Cartier's heart had become stone. Her mind was set on one thing only, and nothing was going to deter her.

Janet disappeared into the plane, and that was it. She was on her way back to New York, while Cartier was left to get the job done.

"Where to now?" Li'l Mama asked.

Cartier remained silent, her attention fixed on the plane down below. She wasn't going anywhere until it took off. She watched the plane push out slowly and taxi its way onto the runaway. And then a few minutes later, it took off into the air back to New York.

Cartier let loose a deep sigh. Now she could leave. She made her way toward the exit and back to the parking garage with Quinn and Li'l Mama right behind her. She hadn't heard from the kidnappers in twenty-four hours. During the last call she'd received from them, she'd been given a chilling reminder: "You have six days, or else I will gut this little brat like a fish."

"Let's get somethin' to eat," Li'l Mama said. "I'm hungry."

Cartier cut her eyes at her. "You can eat at a time like this?"

"What we suppose to do? Just starve ourselves?"

Cartier had heard enough. If Li'l Mama was hungry then — fuck it! — they would go eat and devise this plan to get this money and bring Christian home. Cartier drove out of the parking garage and headed to an airport diner off NW 36th Street.

The girls walked into the quaint establishment with good food and reasonable prices. The girls took a seat at an isolated booth near the windows. There were a handful of diners inside, two couples and several individuals having their meals and reading the daily paper.

Once the girls were seated, one of the waitresses came over with a smile and a hello and placed three menus on the table. "How are y'all ladies doing this afternoon?"

"We fine," Li'l Mama said.

"Welcome to Airport Diner. Would y'all like some coffee or water?" the waitress asked with her catchy smile.

"Coffee for me," Li'l Mama said.

"Same . . . coffee," Quinn said.

Cartier didn't say anything.

The waitress looked at her and asked, "And you, ma'am?"

"Nothin' for me."

The waitress nodded and walked away.

Cartier wanted to distance herself for a moment. She had so many things on her mind, so many hard decisions to make.

The waitress came back with the girls' coffee and asked if they were ready to order.

"Give us a minute," Li'l Mama told her.

"Not a problem."

"Dumb bitch!" Cartier was in such a foul mood, everyone and everything was irritating her. Even the kindness of the waitress. They had their lives, their family, but hers was ripped apart. She didn't care for food, drinks, or cheesy smiles coming from the waitress. She only wanted to go over the plan.

Hector had a home in Palmetto Bay, and from Quinn's mouth, it was a cash and drug haven. At any given time, maybe millions were stashed there, not to mention ki's of cocaine, meth, and ecstasy. Only a select few knew about the home. It was one of two Ghost Ridas' main stash houses in Florida for the drug shipments that came via truck directly off the boat. It was well guarded with high-end security and attack dogs, and on a regular, no less than six men were inside the place handling business and conducting orders. And these men were trained killers, some ex-Marine gangbangers who had returned home from a second or third tour in Iraq and were truly loyal to their clique. And these men didn't play games.

Quinn knew the layout and the extreme risk. The one problem they had was getting within a few feet of the place without raising any suspicion or setting off motion lights and sensors. If you didn't have a reason to be there, then that almost instantly brought death.

Quinn and Li'l Mama dined on roast pork, Greek salad with grilled chicken, and biscuits.

"I don't see any flaws," Li'l Mama said. "We go in, and we ain't comin' back out alive."

Cartier became frustrated. No matter how many ways they looked at it, there just wasn't a way to penetrate that location without any loss of life or creating unwanted attention. Quinn was right when she'd said it was like Fort Knox, but Cartier wasn't going to give up. She had six days to come up with a plan.

Li'l Mama took a bite from her plate and then asked Cartier, "Yo, who's this soldier you got on reserve down here? Where he come from?"

"Don't worry about him. When it happens, I'll make the call."

"It's your call," Li'l Mama replied dryly.

Even though they were cool for the moment, Cartier still had an increasing mistrust for Li'l Mama.

The sun had set, and night swept through the city. Cartier decided to drive down to Palmetto Bay and do her own surveillance of the house and area. She drove, Li'l Mama rode shotgun, and Quinn sat chilling in the backseat. Cartier steered the Avenger through the affluent community slowly, turning onto 156th Street and creeping down the narrow road that snaked through the quiet community of half-a-million-dollar homes with manicured lawns and towering palm trees.

Cartier was coming closer to her mark, which was on her right, a one-story mini compound with a stucco rooftop and no outlet ahead. The landscaping was impeccable. The grass was freshly cut, with a lengthy shoehorn driveway. Parked outside the place was a black BMW X5, a black Infiniti truck, a dark-colored Yukon, and a black Bentley. The stash home blended into the community like green to grass.

Cartier slowed the car down to a crawl and gazed at the compound. There weren't any guards outside, no fences, but there were cameras positioned everywhere. The place was dark, the curtains closed, but the solid oak doors of the front entrance were visible. Near the entrance, there was well-trimmed shrubbery precisely lined up against the smooth stone walls of the house, but it wasn't huge enough to hide behind.

"I told you," Quinn said.

Cartier drove away. "I'm ready to take care of this other problem then," she said.

As the Avenger made its way back to the highway, Li'l Mama and Quinn were quiet.

Cartier pulled out her cell phone and made a call. It was quick. One minute and she was off the phone and focusing back on the dark, winding road, which was almost two miles away from the nearest highway. She took a sudden detour and started driving down an even darker road, SW 72nd Avenue. On both sides were tall trees, wild shrubbery, and darkness. It was isolated to the point of creepy.

Li'l Mama said to Cartier, "Look, I feel like we need to clear the air. I didn't mean to come at you like that, and doubt your judgment."

Cartier glanced at her friend and didn't say anything back as she continued to drive.

Li'l Mama continued with, "You know how much I love you, Cartier. You my sister, and Christian is a daughter to me too. And our friendship means a lot to me. And if I gotta die for you, then —"

Boom!

"Then die, bitch!" Quinn hooted.

The gunfire was loud and disruptive, but Cartier didn't flinch at all. She had given the order, and Quinn didn't hesitate in executing it. She kept her cool, even though Li'l Mama's blood had spattered onto her.

Li'l Mama lay slumped against the bloody door, her body limp like a wet noodle.

"I thought this bitch would never shut the fuck up!" Quinn growled. She had shot Li'l Mama in the back of the head with a .380.

Cartier was deadpan for a moment as she continued to drive down the road. She then pulled over to the side and got out.

Quinn climbed out the backseat with the smoking gun in her hand. She looked to Cartier for their next move. Even though they were in a remote area with a body in the front seat, there was still a chance someone could pass through and become a witness.

Cartier stared at Li'l Mama's corpse, but she didn't seem too concerned. She hated to end this way, but Li'l Mama didn't leave her with any choice.

Moments later, the two ladies saw a pair of headlights approaching and it was the last thing they needed.

"Shit!" Quinn looked like a deer caught in headlights.

The vehicle slowed down. It was an Escalade. It pulled to the side and parked behind them. The door opened, and a black male stepped out.

Quinn hid the pistol behind her back, and was ready to shoot to kill if necessary. Cartier was unruffled, her eyes on the tall stranger walking toward them.

The man approaching had an air of brawn and a strong, magnetic presence. Slender and brown-skinned, he had dark, deep-set eyes and a gleaming bald head, and there was no hair on the chiseled face with two teardrops inked beneath his right eye. He was clad in faded blue jeans, Timberlands, and a stylish black T-shirt, and around his neck hung a long platinum chain and large NY pendant, suggesting he was from up north.

Quinn was instantly attracted to him, but she was afraid she would have to kill him.

Cartier walked toward him. "He's our ride back," she told Quinn.

Quinn dropped the gun to her side.

Mills walked closer to the rented Avenger and saw the body slumped in the passenger seat. It was nothing new to him. He had dropped a few niggas himself.

Cartier was already two steps ahead. The rental car was in Li'l Mama's name. She was the one who rented it and seen in any surveillance videos at the place and nothing traced back to her. It worked out perfectly.

Cartier and Quinn removed their things from the Avenger and wiped it down the best they could. They couldn't afford to leave anything behind. When they felt everything was copacetic, they climbed into the Escalade and sat back, and Mills got behind the wheel and drove away, leaving Li'l Mama to rot on the side of the road like some animal.

Back at the Motel 6, Cartier walked into her room and went straight into the bathroom. There she dropped down to her knees, lifted the toilet seat, hovered her face over the bowl, and threw up chunks. Li'l Mama's death was another tragic moment for her, even though she was the one responsible for ending years of friendship with murder.

❋❋ CHAPTER 18 ❋❋

The young, slender whore kneeled before a butt-naked Hector and moved her mouth near his eight-inch dick as it dangled between his thighs.

He ran his hand through her long, black hair and grabbed the back of her head firmly and pushed her face toward him.

"Suck that shit!" he said sharply.

Softly, she took his dick into her hands and brought the head to her mouth, Hector's hand still clutching the back of her skull. Her full lips wrapped around his hard member, and her tongue touched the slit. He moaned from the warmth of her mouth enveloping him slowly.

She rolled his balls around her fingers and explored his rising erection further with her tongue. She felt his pre-come leaking onto her tongue and continued to suck him faster, licking from the base to the head.

Hector groaned, "Suck that dick. Ooooh, don't stop. Don't fuckin' stop!"

He could feel her thick lips trying to pull the come from his dick, his hand still entangled in her long hair.

She continued to pleasure him with her mouth and tongue, her soft lips sliding down his shaft and back again, doing so meticulously, so he could savor the blissful moment. His eyes closed, he rammed his manhood into her wet mouth, and she started sucking harder and faster, swallowing him whole.

Hector was in the sparsely furnished master bedroom of his four-bedroom Palmetto Bay stash house, his naked ass pressed against the wall as he enjoyed having his dick sucked. His residence was nestled discreetly in the suburbs and away from the hoods of Miami, where his neighbors minded their business, and he kept the location unknown to almost everyone.

The place wasn't furnished for living conditions, but had been turned into a factory somewhat, a drug haven for making a profit, becoming the hub for kilos of cocaine and weed, and heavy quantities of ecstasy moving into Miami and out into different cities. And guns and large amounts of cash were everywhere in the house.

Outside the locked bedroom door his heavily armed goons and soldiers were counting money via counting machines and packaging large quantities of kilos into duffel bags, suitcases, and shopping bags in different rooms of the home. The ki's from the Colombians were for wholesale redistribution to outside crews, their distribution network expanding from Miami into New Orleans, Atlanta, Charlotte, Greenville, South Carolina, and Richmond.

The Ghost Ridas were making close to a hundred thousand a week in drugs, guns, and prostitution. Hector sat on the throne of it all, his hand on the throttle and pushing forward. While his boys were taking care of business outside the bedroom door, he was handling his business in the bedroom.

The chick had a mouth full of dick and grabbed the base of his thickness. She looked up at him while sucking his dick, the room filled with his chanting and moaning.

"Oh shit! Ooh, so fuckin' good."

Hector filled his hand with her full breasts, pinching her hard nipples. She licked, she sucked, and she licked some more. He was ready to shoot his hot come into her mouth.

But he was yearning for other treats. "Yo, go get that shit from out the closet," he told her.

She removed his dick from out her mouth, saliva and pre-come running down her chin, and went over to the closet.

Hector watched her plump ass sashay across the room. Her curves were enticing, and he wanted to peel back her vanilla skin.

She came back to him with the long strap in her hand. Hector smiled. It was definitely playtime for them both.

Both of them positioned themselves on the bed, but Hector was the one that got on all fours, his legs spread. Unbeknownst to his peoples, he was that kind of freak.

The young whore got behind Hector on her knees, slid her finger in his ass, and milked his magic spot.

He cooed, "Ooooh, I like that . . . deeper."

She continued to coax him, rubbing him gently and sucking him from the back. He squirmed with pleasure. The young whore suddenly became the one dominating him. He was now her bitch.

Hector remained on all fours, waiting for his treat.

She harnessed the dildo to her person and neared the plastic penis tip to his awaiting brown hole. Grabbing the KY jelly, she lubricated his backside. And then with him facedown and ass up, she slid the sexual toy into him from behind and worked his spot, thrusting the hard toy dick into him.

"Fuck me!" Hector cried out.

The two were in a heated moment, losing themselves in one twisted bliss. But the sounds of sirens and glaring lights seen in a distance from the bedroom window made them stop suddenly. He jumped to his feet and reached for his clothing. He pulled up his pants and became alert. Hearing cops around his primary stash house was never a good thing.

He marched out of the bedroom in his jeans, shirtless, his gang tattoos exposed proudly like military insignia. His peoples were on high alert, heavily armed and bracing themselves for the worst.

But the lights went flying by his place.

"What the fuck!" he uttered. He stepped outside onto the manicured lawn. Something was wrong. Something had happened, and it happened close by. He could see the police racing, their engines roaring and going the other way. They weren't coming for him. It was a slight relief.

He lingered on the lawn for a moment, gazing at the direction the marked car went toward, somewhere near the marsh, not too far from his stash house. He needed to know what was happening, even if it wasn't his business. One could never be too careful. He was at war with the Miami Gotti Boys and couldn't be caught slipping.

He went back into the house and said, "Yo, Tumble, get the car. We gon' check this out."

Tumble nodded and went to get the keys to the truck.

A half hour later, Tumble came to a stop a few feet from heavy police activity on SW 72nd Avenue. Going farther down wasn't feasible; the cops had shut it down. The dark road, cluttered with towering trees and thick shrubbery, was suddenly lit up by several police lights. It was obvious there was something found half mile down the road, and that homicide was on the scene doing an investigation.

Tumble stepped out the truck and walked down, leaving Hector seated in the passenger seat, smoking his cigar and watching the commotion from afar. He walked toward the yellow tape and kept a keen eye down the road. Other motorists had stopped short, being nosy. Tumble found out what he could from them and then walked back to the SUV.

He climbed inside and said to Hector, "They found a body in some car . . . some bitch."

"What?"

"Yeah. Bitch dead, son."

Hector didn't like the sound of that. It was where his business was, and having the police around made him paranoid. "Yo, we out."

"Back to the house?"

"Yeah. Then we packin' shit up an' leavin' there."

Tumble looked dumbfounded. "Why?"

"I got a bad feeling. Besides, you know how we do. We don't stay in one location too long. We at war, Tumble. Fuck that! I ain't taking no chances."

Tumble nodded. He made a U-turn in the SUV and went back in the direction they came from.

Detective Sharp stopped his Dodge Charger just short of the crime scene on the remote road. He stepped out under the canopy of stars and looked ahead. He had been called in to another homicide, miles away from the glitz and glamour of South Beach, and also the war-torn hoods farther north. He wasn't the primary detective in this case, but he was told there might be a link to the other cases he was investigating. He trekked toward the crime scene coolly, maneuvered toward the car with the body in it, and was updated quickly.

"Black female, late twenties or early thirties, gunshot to the back of her head," another detective said.

Sharp moved closer to the car and looked intently at the body inside. CSI was all over it, taking pictures. It was ugly. Whoever did this wasn't new at murder. It was obviously premeditated.

Sharp stared closer at the slumped body, inspecting everything around the car. The police were dusting for fingerprints and had found another set of tire tracks in the dirt behind the car. From the size of the tire marks, the detectives guessed that it was a bigger vehicle, an SUV.

"You have a name on her?" Sharp asked.

"Not at the moment. She had no ID on her, and this is a Rent-a-Car. We're running the plates and everything now."

Detective Sharp looked into her face acutely, and there was a hint of recognition for a moment. "I've seen this woman before."

"Where?"

He examined her closer. He had a photographic memory. "I can't place it yet."

"Well, she was a very beautiful woman," the other detective said, "what's left of her anyway."

Sharp ignored his comment and went into his covert mood. He tuned everything out and painstakingly inspected the area. As he looked around, it suddenly dawned on him that she was at an earlier crime scene comforting a woman named Cartier. Either Cartier was the unluckiest woman to be around with all her loved ones dropping like flies, or, she was the mastermind behind all this carnage. Detective Sharp was determined to unravel the truth. His first priority now was to locate Cartier, deliver the bad news, and ask her a few questions.

❈❆ CHAPTER 19 ❆❈

With five days until the deadline for the ransom, Cartier was ready to rob a bank, do a heist, anything to come up with the million dollars. She now wanted desperately to reach back out to Head back in New York, but she knew that was a risk she couldn't take.

Even with Mills on her team, they were still short on manpower. But Cartier needed to pull it off, even if they had to run into the crib Scarface-style with their guns blazing and kill whoever.

Mills sat at the ring-shaped table in the hotel room with several pistols displayed in front of him, inspecting and cleaning the guns, looking like a professional assassin with his tools for murder. Clad in a T-shirt, his lean, muscular frame was impressive. And he seemed very skilled with the guns in front of him. He removed the clips and took the barrels apart. Cleaning and maintaining his equipment was not only the key to increasing a weapon's lifespan, but it was necessary to ensure safe operation. There wasn't anything worse than a gun jamming on someone while in a threatening situation.

Cartier watched Mills at work. He had a .357 Magnum in his hand. He tied an old sock around the rear cylinder opening to protect the revolver from damage when the bore brush got pushed through the barrel. He dipped the bore brush in cleaning solvent and went to work on his equipment. Then he took a cleaning patch and dipped it in cleaning solvent then fed it all the way through the barrel of the gun. He repeated this action a few times before using a toothbrush to clean around the muzzle of the gun. He then used a little more cleaning solvent on the rear cylinder opening. Using the brush again and some cleaning solvent, he brushed the outside and the ends of the cylinders. After he was done, the .357 Magnum looked like pure perfection.

Mills had several more pistols to inspect and clean. He was only nineteen, but a skilled and deadly killer. His eyes were cold and his voice raspy. He didn't speak much, but they always said you had to watch out for the silent ones.

Cartier needed some air. She stepped out the room for a moment onto the exterior hallway and gazed at the city before her. It was mid-afternoon, and the sky was clear. She smoked a cigarette, waiting for Quinn to show up. They had mapped a plan together. It took them hours of thinking and brainstorming to converge on one possible solution that wouldn't get them all killed. And what they came up with could work. But there wasn't any room for error. They had to be meticulous and on point.

Quinn didn't want Hector anywhere around the stash house at all. They figured a total of six to ten men had to occupy the residence. The scary part about their scheme was not knowing how many armed goons they had to deal with once inside. Their number was only an estimate.

Cartier took a few deep pulls from the Newport between her fingers. She was shaky and nervous. Every day she thought about her daughter. Every day she went off somewhere alone and cried her heart out.

She leaned over the railing, lingering in her crushing thoughts. She took one final pull from the cigarette and flicked it over the railing. Then she went back into the room where Mills was still focused on cleaning his pistols. He was working on the third. She took a seat on the bed and waited for Quinn to show up.

Half an hour later, there was a knock at the door. Mills stood up. He picked up the fully loaded .357 Magnum, which was now gleaming, and gestured for Cartier to remain seated on the bed. He walked toward the door cautiously with gun in hand and peeped through the small hole centered in the door.

"It's Quinn," they both heard.

Mills opened up.

Quinn rushed into the room saying, "We got a problem."

Cartier stood up. "What now?"

"My brother got spooked an' uprooted everythin' in that house last night an' left."

"What the fuck you talkin' about, Quinn?"

"The cops found Li'l Mama's body near his place. We fucked up. He got spooked an' made his move. The place is empty."

"Fuck me!" Cartier shouted. "This isn't happening!"

"It is."

"You know where to?"

"I have no idea."

Overwhelmed with stress, Cartier just wanted to drop down on her knees and cry. It was Murphy's Law in her book — what can go wrong will go wrong.

Mills stood quietly with a deadpan expression. His only task down in Miami was to be Cartier's muscle and help out. If she said go, he would go, and go with brute force.

"We need another plan," Quinn said.

Cartier went over to the table where the guns were displayed. She picked up a 9mm and out of the blue pointed it at Quinn and scowled.

"What the fuck are you doin', Cartier?" Quinn exclaimed.

"You lyin' to me, Quinn?" Cartier asked through clenched teeth. "You sure you ain't makin' this shit up so we can stray away from the plan? After all, he is your brother."

"This is no fuckin' lie, Cartier. He's gone!" Quinn spat back, not looking the least bit intimidated by the gun in her face.

Mills minded his business and chose not to intervene. If Cartier shot Quinn, then he would help clean up the mess. Miami was temporary for him anyway.

Quinn looked at Mills. His eyes were cold and callous. And for some strange reason, it turned her on.

Cartier frowned at Quinn. Paranoia was on overtime for her. It would be like plucking wings off a fly if she killed Quinn, because after losing Li'l Mama, who was her best friend, Quinn was second-rate.

"Get that fuckin' gun out my face, Cartier," Quinn growled.

Cartier locked eyes with her. She lowered the gun. She didn't kill her only because she needed her. Quinn still knew the right locations to hit up and the dealers to stick up.

"What now?" Cartier asked herself, almost looking defeated.

With five days to come up with the money, worry was definitely settling in.

Cartier said, "Fuck it! We turn this city inside out and rob whoever we can. Pimps, drug dealers, everybody, I don't give a fuck!" She looked at Mills, who didn't respond. She added, "We smart. We know the game. We do what we gotta do to get this money. We cause havoc on these muthafuckas in Miami, 'cuz I'm gettin' my fuckin' daughter back."

With four days left, Cartier hadn't heard any word from the kidnappers or her daughter. She yearned to hear Christian's voice, to see and kiss her again, to wrap her arms around her little girl. Cartier wanted nothing more but to have Christian return to her and leave Miami as soon as possible. The experience had become a long, drawn-out nightmare for her.

Cartier sat behind the wheel of her Range Rover in South Beach, parked in front of the Gap store on Collins Avenue. Quinn and Mills sat incognito in a separate car. The sun-drenched day was vibrant with shoppers and inhabitants. She eyed the front entrance like a hawk while smoking a cigarette. The street was lined with shops like Armani Exchange, Steve Madden, and Urban Outfitters, towering palm trees decorating the trendy strip. This was where the affluent of Miami came to spend their days and nights. Business was good, from the stylish boutiques to the trendsetting sneaker stores.

Once, on days like today, Cartier would indulge herself in shopping sprees, spas, and sipping on maté. But those days were long gone. Cartier was a different woman, becoming more ruthless and uncaring. The malice building inside of her was manifested through her frosty eyes, prickly attitude, and deadly ways. She had transformed into The Terminator, her focal point rooted on two things — money and revenge. She hadn't smiled in what felt like forever.

Cartier watched a blonde woman exit a Chanel store with a few shopping bags in her hands. The leggy redbone was wearing a black-and-white mini dress. She screamed wealth as she walked around South Beach with a Platinum Card attached to her hand. Quinn had pointed her out, and Cartier was ready to attack.

This bitch was Cartier's mark, but it was her husband that Cartier and Quinn wanted to go after. His name was Domea, a well-known drug dealer from Little Haiti who pushed kilos of cocaine and marijuana. He had relations with the Miami Gotti Boys and was known to be a baller and shot-caller. Cartier was ready to set him up, run into his crib, duct-tape his wife and kids, and rob him for everything he had, but she needed to follow his bitch around first. Domea kept his residence hush-hush, but it was his bitch that they were about to kidnap, pistol-whip if they had to, and have her give up the information and loot.

Cartier watched the blonde bitch strut down the street in her high heels, looking carefree. She already hated her. *Why is my life in fuckin' shambles, and this bitch has the fuckin' world at her feet?* Cartier was about to step out her Range Rover and follow the blonde bitch, but the minute her red-bottoms hit the street, a suit-and-tie-wearing detective walked up to her, putting a critical dent into her plans.

"Cartier, may I have a word with you? I'm Detective Sharp. You remember me?"

Cartier scowled. "No! I'm busy."

"I just need five minutes of your time."

Cartier watched her prey strut away down Collins Avenue and disappear in the afternoon crowd. This bitch-ass cop was fucking up her livelihood. She needed to do this robbery. "What the fuck you want?" she hissed.

"Listen, cut the hostility. Do you remember me?"

Cartier glared at him. At first there was no recognition, but then it came to her. "You were that detective at my place the night my family was killed."

He nodded.

"Any leads yet?" she asked nonchalantly.

"We are still working on it."

"Whatever."

Cartier wondered how he found her. But it was irrelevant. She had more important things to worry about. Her body language clearly showed she didn't want to be bothered with the detective and his questions.

Sharp looked into her eyes. "Your friend, the one at your apartment with you. Have you seen her?"

Cartier's stomach dropped. "What?"

"If my memory recalls correctly, you had two friends with you when you discovered the bodies."

"Yeah, and?"

"Where is she?"

"Why the fuck do you care?"

"When was the last time you saw her, Ms. Timmons? Or would you prefer 'Mrs. Timmons-Payne'?"

"Look jump to the point 'cuz I ain't got all fucking day." Cartier cut her eyes. "Yeah, my last name is/was Timmons-Payne. My husband Jason Payne was murdered, but my guess is you already know that. And if you think that I had a hand in that then you need to turn in your badge because you're a dumbass detective."

"Did you?"

"Did I what?"

"Have a hand in your girlfriend's murder."

Cartier didn't even blink. "What are you talking about?"

"We have an unidentified body sitting in the morgue and I'm almost certain she runs in your circle. A circle that's growing smaller by the day."

Cartier ignored his sarcasm. He was trying to rattle her and it wasn't working.

"Look, where is this goin'? I'm the victim here, so why are you talkin' to me like I'm some suspect?"

"I'm just doing my job and trying to put the pieces together, and in time, everything will make sense. All those involved will be prosecuted to the fullest extent of the law, which in Miami means people could get the death penalty. Male or female . . . no one is exempt."

"Are you threatening me, Detective Sharp?"

"Just doing a thorough investigation. And another thing —" Detective Sharp pulled out a photograph from his suit jacket, a picture of Li'l Mama lying naked on the slab in the morgue. "This is a friend of yours, right?"

Cartier remained blank looking at the photo. Li'l Mama's face was swollen and almost unrecognizable.

"She was found shot to death in a car in Palmetto Bay the other night. I find it ironic that your friend was just with you no more than two weeks ago and is found murdered right after your family."

"What are you inquiring, Detective Sharp? It's fuckin' sad. I had love for her. We grew up together in Brooklyn, but she was a wild girl, went out to do her own thang, started hangin' wit' a rough crew. I couldn't tell her shit."

"So you say, but you don't look too heartbroken about her death."

"Look, where I come from, people get bodied every day. Li'l Mama wasn't the only friend I lost that way, and she damn sure won't be the last. Yes, I'm sad, but my family has been brutally murdered, Detective Sharp. And instead of coming to me wit' this bullshit and questioning me about a friend's murder, why don't you go out and do ya fuckin' job and find out who killed the ones I love!"

Cartier was becoming fed up. She was ready to depart from the cop. She didn't know who was watching her. The questions were trying her last nerve. And Detective Sharp didn't have any physical evidence to link her to any of the crimes, nor could he contradict her story about her friend.

Cartier spun on her heels and climbed back into her Range Rover. She was ready to spit in the cops' face, but thought against it. She couldn't afford to get locked up. That would be precious time gone, and her daughter would definitely be dead. She started the ignition and drove away, leaving Detective Sharp staring at the back of the vehicle.

Detective Sharp looked at his partner Lam and smiled. "We good?"

"Like a sunny day," Lam returned

Unbeknownst to Cartier, while Sharp had her attention, Detective Lam had subtly placed a tracking device underneath the chariot of her truck. It was unconstitutional because it wasn't court ordered and she was only a suspect, but he just wanted to keep tabs on her until he got a solid lead.

Quinn had seen Cartier caught up with that detective in front of the Chanel store, and decided to take charge. She and Mills followed the cocaine-colored Benz truck as it moved down Collins Avenue. They were on the vehicle like white on rice. They couldn't lose the bitch because she was critical to their plan tonight. Collins Avenue was dense with traffic and pedestrians, making it difficult to keep up with the truck, but Quinn maneuvered through the streets, remaining two cars behind the Benz like a professional. It was as if she'd done this before.

Mills sat silent in the passenger seat, a 9mm on his lap. He was being observant, remembering streets, landmarks, and faces. He was ready for some action, and the way things were playing out, it seemed to be coming soon.

Quinn followed the Benz for several blocks. They had to be precise because there wasn't any room for errors. And if they pulled this heist off correctly, it was going to be the first of many in the next few days.

"Stupid, naïve bitch," she uttered. "These dumb bitches make it too easy for us in this game."

"Where you think she's goin'?" Mills asked.

"I have no idea. But she's gonna stop somewhere, an' we gon' be there when she does."

Quinn glanced at Mills. She had a heavy attraction toward him. His thuggish mannerism made her pussy wet. He sat back in the truck looking cool and was mostly quiet. He seemed to be about his business. His Brooklyn accent and cold eyes made her want to jump on his lap and devour him like some sweet candy. But there wasn't anything sweet about Mills. She definitely wanted to fuck him. It had been a long minute since she had some dick. And Mills seemed to be the perfect candidate to scratch her much-needed itch. But it was business before pleasure.

A few miles from South Beach now, they continued to follow the Benz as it crossed the Venetian Causeway. They were one car behind the showy vehicle, but still remained discreet. Quinn wasn't going to lose Domea's blonde, big-titty bitch.

As Quinn drove, her cell phone rang. Cartier's name showed on the caller ID screen. She answered.

"Y'all on that bitch?"

"Yeah, we still on her," Quinn replied.

"Good."

"What's up wit' you an' the detective? What he wanted?"

"He was just in my business. Wanna ask some questions, but fuck him!"

Quinn had a funny feeling about that, but she didn't push it.

"Anyway, stay on that bitch and hit me up and let me know what's up."

"Okay." Quinn hung up.

They soon found themselves in North Miami, a city located in the northeast of Miami-Dade County, about ten miles north of Miami and resting on Biscayne Bay. Mostly blacks and Latinos lived there. Quinn knew the area. She figured the only reason Domea's bitch was coming out this far was to hide something from her husband.

The Benz truck made a few turns, traveling deeper into the city, and then pulled into a curved driveway of a well-kept one-story home on a quiet residential block. The front yard was jumbled with coconut trees and trimmed shrubbery. Domea's bitch pulled up and parked behind a black Porsche Cayenne in the driveway.

Quinn slowly drove by the home as the sexy little woman stepped out of her ride looking stunning in her black-and-white mini, her long, sensuous blonde hair flowing down to her back. She had more curves on her than a racetrack.

Quinn said, "We onto somethin'."

Mills remained stoic. He gripped the 9mm. When it was his time to act, he wasn't going to hesitate. He lit a Newport and looked around the area, which was a far contrast from his Brooklyn home. The days in Miami were sun-drenched and hot, and the players and goons were a force to be reckoned with. Mills knew not to underestimate anyone. And since his arrival, he'd been hearing about the Ghost Ridas and the Miami Gotti Boys warring with each other. Their war or beef wasn't his business, until it became his business. He was only in Miami to do a favor for Cartier on Apple's behalf.

Quinn parked her ride a half block down from the residence and watched the activity from the driver's-side mirror. The blonde woman strutted toward the front entrance of the home and rang the bell. Soon after, a shirtless, chiseled man with cornrows and gang tattoos across his body stepped out and pulled her into his arms.

Quinn smiled. "What we got here?"

The woman went inside and the door closed. It was evident from the steamy greeting that the two were going to be a moment inside.

Quinn looked at Mills and said to him, "Your turn — Do what you do. We don't have much time left."

Mills nodded. He shoved the pistol into his waistband, concealing it, and exited the truck. He discreetly walked toward the one-story residence and moved stealthily into the backyard. He had plenty of shade, shrubbery, and trees to hide behind. It was a nice-size home with a one-car garage and an in-ground pool in the backyard.

A warm summer day sometimes meant open windows, but Mills had another method of entering the house. He scaled the wooden fence and made his way into the backyard, crouching near the foundation and moving toward the door. He had been breaking into homes and businesses in Brooklyn since he was ten years old. Miami was just newer territory for him. This area was more laid-back, with no bars on the windows or dogs in the yard.

Mills knew that most locks around the house were simple pin tumbler locks and could be relatively easy to open using a pick and torsion wrench. It took a great deal of skill and patience. He went to work on the lock, inserting a thin metal pin into the back door and moving the pin around until he heard a click. The door eased open like he had his own key.

He removed the pistol from his waistband and slowly made his way inside. He crept through the kitchen and entered the hallway. The afternoon sunlight illuminated every corner of the house. The well-furnished place was carpeted, so he didn't have to worry about any loose or squeaky floorboards.

With his arm outstretched and the pistol at the end of it, Mills cautiously made his way toward one of the four bedrooms down the hallway. As he walked stealthily, he could hear a woman's moans from one of the bedrooms. It was the perfect opportunity.

The first bedroom he passed was empty. The second was too. He made his way toward the master bedroom. The woman's moans grew louder, and he heard the man grunting.

"Fuck me, nigga! Ooooh, fuck me! Fuck me with that big black dick! Ooooh, yes!"

The door of the master bedroom was ajar. Mills crept closer and took a look inside. The couple was fucking doggy-style, and glistening in sweat, their backs to the door. He witnessed the man's hairy ass pound against the curvy redbone bitch from the back, her face pushed into the pillows and her ass arched, cheeks spread. Her body was luscious and thick, and she was taking his dick like she was Wonder Woman. The man gripped her hips and pulled her long blonde hair like they were reins to a horse.

"Oh shit! Fuck me, muthafucka!" she howled.

Mills watched the man thrust. Then the man withdrew himself almost completely and then thrust into her again. His back was swathed with gangland tattoos — "Miami Gotti Boys 305" was inked across his back.

"Ooooooh shit! Give me that good pussy! Give me that good pussy! You feel so good!"

Mills wasn't there to see a peepshow. He was there to handle his business. He treaded farther into the bedroom, the 9mm trained on the man's back. He smirked and said loudly, "Damn! That's fuckin' nice."

Abruptly, the man jumped out of the pussy and spun around. The blonde bitch shrieked when she saw the tall stranger with a gun aimed at them.

The man shouted, "Yo, what the fuck?"

Mills stepped closer and fired. *Bak!*

The bullet tore through his chest and ripped open his heart. He dropped dead in the prone position instantly. The woman screamed louder, retreating in fear.

Mills approached closer with a deadly scowl. "Bitch, shut the fuck up and sit ya ass down before I murder ya ass too!"

She pulled the bedroom sheets up to her neck, trying to cover her nakedness.

Mills kept the 9mm trained at her head as he made the phone call. He gazed at the frightened woman, tears streaming down her face and horror showing in her eyes, her moment of bliss unexpectedly transformed into a living hell.

The phone rang, and Quinn picked up.

"It's me. I got this nervous bitch," he said.

"A'ight."

Mills took a seat at the edge of the bed. He removed a cigarette from a pack of Newport he found on the dresser, lit it, and took a much-needed drag. As he smoked, he looked down at the body. Blood started to pool around it, leaving a crimson stain on the cream flooring.

He said to her, "That dick was gettin' good, right? I saw y'all."

The woman looked sickened and befuddled.

"You might as well get comfortable, 'cuz you gonna be here for a moment."

❈ CHAPTER 20 ❈

Cartier and Quinn strutted into Wall Nightclub on Collins Avenue like a pair of luscious twin divas, wearing the same outfits — slinky thin-strapped minidresses with criss-cross, low-cut backs, Cartier in red and Quinn in black. They instantly caught the attention of everyone in the place as they made their way toward the bar for drinks to Drake's "Crew Love."

The ladies were on a mission. They had seventy-two hours left. It was do or die, take no prisoners. Cartier was in a zone and thoroughly focused, detached from the partying in the club. Quinn was the same way. The patrons were like live wires in the retro cool club with the long black bar, its many VIP areas, and a large classic gold couch in the middle of the club. The ladies ordered two Long Island Iced Teas and began observing their surroundings. The ballers were in the house in swarms. The VIP areas were all taken, with niggas bejeweled in platinum and big-face watches, looking like trendsetters and popping bottles like it was New Year's Eve.

Dolled up and looking glamorous, Quinn and Cartier were pure eye candy. The bitches were hating, and niggas gawked at them from head to toe, thirsty to grasp their attention.

"Love, can I buy you a drink?" one man offered.

"Damn! Y'all lookin' too fuckin' sexy," another slim hood said.

"Yo, beautiful, let me get this dance with you."

"Damn, I see heaven is missing two of its angels," another joked.

The catcalls came from every direction, but Quinn and Cartier weren't interested. They had an agenda and little time to pull it off. The men coming at them weren't worth their time.

"We can buy our own drinks," Quinn spat back at one annoying young dude who didn't look like he had two pennies to rub together.

"You can't afford us, so fuck off!" Cartier chimed.

"Damn! It's like that? Why y'all stink bitches actin' so fuckin' stuck-up?"

Cartier shot a murderous look at him. She wasn't in any mood for games or ignorance. The little nigga was barking up the wrong tree. He caught the hint right away and stepped off, his pride crushed.

Cartier took a sip from her drink and observed the VIP areas. There they were, the ballers, the shot-callers, all occupying the VIP booths with their icy jewels and cocky attitudes, surrounded by their entourage and groupies. It was the ladies' mission to attract their attention. And they knew how to.

"Let's do this," Quinn said with a smile.

Quinn strutted away, moving through the crowd and toward the dance floor like a fall breeze. Cartier followed behind her. The dance floor was flooded with patrons grinding and moving to J Rand's "Up Against the Wall," its raunchy lyrics pouring out from the speakers.

Quinn started moving to the beat of the song, and once she stepped onto the dance floor, she went in, gyrating and winding her hips to the beat, showing natural rhythm in her stilettos. She slowly touched herself, leisurely moving her manicured hands across her figure, from her thighs up to her breasts. It was like she was selling sex to everyone. She moved like she was alone in her bedroom, closing her eyes and forgetting she was surrounded by people. She didn't care who was watching as she twisted and turned with her slick, mesmerizing moves.

Cartier followed suit. It was her turn to show and shake what her mama gave her. She dropped down to the floor eagle-style and bounced back up, her sexy attire revealing flesh and thighs. Her salacious moves caused niggas to stop and watch like they were in the strip clubs. Cartier started to bounce her ass up and down, and then she positioned her hand beneath her minidress and touched herself, enticing those who were watching.

Continuing her dirty-dancing routine, she moved closer to Quinn and pulled her juicy backside against her pelvis, and the two became entwined like vines wrapped around each other in heated rhythm, gyrating against each other seductively. There was touching and feeling and seductive looks.

Face to face, bumping and grinding passionately, they looked over at one of the ballers seated in the VIP area and smiled heavily. Cartier had her eyes on one particular baller, Domea, who sat among his goons in the secluded area. The table in front of him cluttered with bottles of Moët, rosé, Cristal, and Patrón Platinum. He was flanked by a young caramel brunette in a tight white dress, but his eyes were fixed on the sexy interaction between Quinn and Cartier.

Cartier noticed him watching from the corner of her eye. She had him hook, line, and sinker. He rose up from his seated position and stared at them, forgetting about the young bitch up under him. Cartier turned the heat up. With her dress riding up her thighs, she thrust herself into Quinn and ran her hands across Quinn's breasts, while Quinn continued to gyrate her backside into her.

The DJ even shouted them out. "Yo, yo, yo, yo! The ladies in the red and black matching dresses, y'all gonna end up gettin' this club shut down if y'all keep dancing like that!" he hollered through the mic. "But fuck it! Get us shut down tonight! I'm lovin' what I'm seein' down there!"

Quinn and Cartier smiled.

Domea was looking fresh in his Hall white shirt under a black tanner vest, and sporting denim, a dark washed driver hat, and a Bentley watch gleaming around his wrist.

Quinn and Cartier smiled at him, and he smiled right back. He was lost in their spicy performance, fading out everything and everyone around him. It was coming soon, they knew it. It was the same cliché with these balling muthafuckas.

Domea called one of his cronies over and whispered something in his ear. The man nodded and stepped away.

Cartier and Quinn had to be nonchalant. For the moment, it was about them on the dance floor, until the moment came when it wasn't about them. As the girls danced, looking like horny young temptresses, and teasing so many wide-eyed men around them, a tall, lean figure in a silk button-down and black fedora pushed his way through the crowd, headed in their direction.

He walked up to Cartier and shouted into her ear, wrestling with the blaring music. "Hello. My name is Russell, and I have someone that yearns for a moment of your time. He thinks you are gorgeous and wants the both of you to accompany him in the VIP area." His English was proper, and his attire said money.

Nonchalantly, Cartier asked, "Who?"

He pointed in Domea's direction. Domea raised the bottle of Moët in his hand and nodded at the lovely ladies.

"He's cute. But tell your friend we don't come cheap."

Russell chuckled. "We don't do cheap, mama. We only fuck with top-of-the-line brands."

The ladies chuckled, going along with the plan, flirting and playing hard-to-get, but not too hard. They soon agreed to join Domea in his circle of luxury.

Following behind Russell, Quinn and Cartier were going into phase two of their plan. They strutted behind the towering, well-dressed figure in their stilettos and received endless hate from other bitches watching.

Domea stood and greeted the ladies once they were in his domain. "Ladies, what's happening, what's happening?" He shook both ladies' hands. "Y'all put on one hell of a performance. I felt I owed y'all something."

Quinn chuckled. "We just came out to have some fun."

"And fun it is." Domea eyed Quinn up and down with a wayward smile. "We all came out to have some fun. Let's definitely have some fun." He then looked at Cartier in the same manner. His lust for them was evident.

Quinn and Cartier continued to act like two airhead bitches, with their flirtatious smiles and bubbly chuckling.

"Where y'all from?" Domea asked.

"Miami," Quinn answered.

Cartier told him, "Philly."

"Philly, huh? Long way from home."

"I know. But I love Miami."

"Yeah, there's a lot to love out here — the city, the beaches, the money, and me."

"I see that." Cartier smiled.

"Y'all have a seat. Get comfortable. The 'Doublemint Twins' are in the building. I like. I definitely like."

Cartier and Quinn quickly flanked Domea on the soft velvet seats.

The young brunette he'd been with earlier promptly caught an attitude with both ladies as she was forced to move from her position. She sucked her teeth and scowled at them. "Bitches!"

Quinn frowned at her, but it wasn't about her, it was about sticking to the plan.

Domea put a glass filled with rosé in both ladies' hands and encouraged them to drink up. Flanked by Quinn and Cartier, he felt like a king. He placed his hand on their smooth, exposed thighs and began fondling them.

"Yeah, we definitely are partying tonight," he said pompously, giving both ladies his attention.

Quinn and Cartier weren't trying to get tipsy or drunk, so they watched their alcohol consumption. Besides, they were moderate drinkers.

But the one thing they couldn't control at the moment was Domea's hands. He was all over them, showing them who was the boss. His hands moved between Cartier's short dress and Quinn's plump backside. They allowed the groping to continue, but inside, Cartier wanted to break his fucking arm.

Two in the morning and many drinks later, Domea and his crew exited the club in high spirits. He had his arms around Quinn and Cartier like a pimp as he walked toward the silver Benz G-Class SUV with the driver waiting. The trio climbed into the backseat, where Domea expected the party to continue, getting into some freaky shit. He had plans to fuck both ladies while sniffing cocaine off their breasts. They were too sexy to fuck sober.

His goons jumped into a black Escalade and followed behind.

Domea became an octopus in the backseat. The girls laughed along with Domea as the SUV made its way to the nearest main road. His eyes lit up like stars with so much flesh showing in his presence.

"Take y'all panties off," he said with a mischievous grin.

"Ummm, so it's that kind of party?" Quinn asked.

"Yes, it is."

They had to play along until the time came, so they tolerated Domea's kisses on their necks, breasts, and thighs.

His hand traveled up Cartier's dress, where he pushed his fingers into her shaved pussy. She cringed for a moment but allowed his slim fingers to roll around inside of her. He rubbed her clit gently and said, "I can't wait for this."

"I can't either," Cartier replied with a counterfeit smile.

Quinn wasn't immune to Domea's wandering hands and shameless mannerisms. His hand slid underneath her dress too, fingering her pretty pussy. He leaned forward, cupping her tits, and placed his mouth onto her chocolate nipples and sucked them like they were lemon drops.

She cooed, "Ay, *papi.*"

The Benz SUV traveled north on the way to a more affluent section of the city as the party was getting started in the backseat. Domea was eager to get between one of the ladies' smooth, thick legs and start fucking. His pants were unzipped, and his hard-on was showing. He grabbed for Cartier again. He wanted to fuck her first.

But just then, his cell phone rang. He looked at the caller ID and saw it was his wife calling. He raised himself up from being pressed against Cartier to answer his phone. "Excuse me, ladies," he said. "I need to take this."

Cartier and Quinn already knew the deal. It was game time.

"Hey, baby," he said.

The voice on the other end said, "I got ya bitch, and if you do anything stupid, I'll tear her apart piece by piece — I promise you that."

"What? Who the fuck is this?"

"Domea, help me!" his wife cried out of the blue. "Help me!"

"Felicia! Felicia!" Domea hollered.

The caller said, "Don't fuck wit' us!"

Suddenly Domea's mood changed.

Before Domea could say anything else, Cartier had her hand in her purse and pulled out the snub-nosed .38 revolver and pressed it against his temple. "You flinch, you die," she said through clenched teeth.

"What the fuck!"

The driver, becoming nervous, started to swerve between lanes.

Cartier said, "Tell your driver to relax. There's no need to get nervous."

"Tommy, relax," Domea said calmly. "We gonna be all right."

The driver nodded.

Quinn told him, "Now this is the plan — we go to your home, you open up the safe, and we leave wit' a sizeable donation."

"So y'all bitches is fuckin' robbin' me?"

"It's been a long time coming. You have lots of cash available, and it's time to share the wealth."

"Fuck you!"

"No! Fuck *you*!" Cartier spat back, "And unless you want ya wife dead, then I suggest you do what the fuck ya told. And I tell you right now, before she's murdered, I got a big daddy-long-dick muthafucka that's gonna rape her like it ain't shit."

Domea seemed ready to cooperate.

"First, we need you to make another phone call," Quinn said.

Domea picked up his phone and dialed Russell, his right-hand man, who was following them in the Escalade, unaware of what was happening. As Domea dialed the number, Quinn shoved the gun into his crotch. It was a stern warning to shut his mouth and follow procedure.

The phone rang, and Russell picked up. "Yeah. What's up?"

"Russell, y'all niggas fall back. I'm good."

"You sure?

"Yeah, these bitches are fuckin' freaky. I'll call you later if I need anything."

"A'ight."

The Benz SUV came to a stop at a red light. Then the Escalade came to a stop right next to it at the same red light.

Cartier put her face into Domea's lap, pretending she was giving him a blowjob.

Quinn twisted the revolver into his groin, causing him to cringe. "Don't fuck wit' us," she said. "You be cool now, ay."

The passenger window to the Escalade came rolling down, and Russell gazed into the dimly lit backseat suspiciously.

Quinn became that bubbly, chuckling bimbo again. Her dress was in disarray, and she rubbed her hands on Domea like she was ready to get nasty.

Russell looked Domea in the eyes. "You sure you okay, boss?" he asked.

Cartier popped her head up from Domea's lap. "Hey, boys," she said, all smiles.

As Quinn smiled at Russell, she continued to twist and turn the snub-nosed barrel into Domea's groin.

"Yeah, I said I'm fuckin' okay," Domea hollered. "Just leave us."

Russell nodded.

When the light changed to green, the Escalade went in a different direction. Quinn and Cartier were relieved, but they weren't out the hot water yet. The man continued to drive. He was nervous, but he wasn't trying to be a hero.

"I swear, y'all fuckin' bitches —"

Cartier smashed the revolver against Domea's face, drawing blood. "Shut the fuck up!" she shouted. The hit was personal, some slight revenge for his groping and touching throughout the night.

"Ah shit! You broke my fuckin' nose, bitch!" he screamed, clutching his face.

Cartier hit him again. She wanted to show him who was in control.

The driver remained calm and continued driving. The last thing he wanted was a gunshot to the back of his head. He steadied his eyes on the road and kept under the speed limit.

The Benz SUV rolled up to an ultimate retreat bay front treasure nestled among a forest of swaying palm trees. The lavish residence was outlined by exquisite gardens and a koi pond. It was a sophisticated home with impeccable style.

"Fuck me!" Cartier said in awe.

They knew Domea was rich, but they didn't think he was this filthy rich. Cartier instructed the driver to move closer to the front door. They were in enemy territory, and there was no telling what kind of surprises was waiting for them.

With the gun pressed to the back of his head, they instructed Domea to slowly step out the vehicle. The driver stepped out also. Cautiously, the ladies pushed the men into the home.

"Who's home?" Cartier asked.

"No one."

Cartier pressed the gun to the back of his head angrily. "You better not be lying to us."

"I'm not fuckin' lyin'. We're alone."

The ladies took in the lavish home with its two-story rotunda illuminating cupola, vaulted ceiling, security doors, and private terrace. The place also had a wine cellar, theater, and a Tensui water purifier for the entire house.

Domea led the ladies to his safe, which was located in the walk-in closet in the master bedroom. He removed some clothes, pushed a button, and the wall to the closet slid back, revealing bundles of money and jewelry.

"Bingo!" Cartier grinned.

Domea was forced down on his knees, the snub-nosed still pressed to the back of his head.

Cartier started to empty out the safe. She threw everything into a bag they found in the house. They planned on leaving him dry.

"Y'all bitches satisfied? 'Cuz I guarantee y'all won't live long enough to spend a fuckin' dime."

Cartier said, "Yeah? Well, fuck you too!"

Pop!

She put a bullet into the back of Domea's head, and he tumbled over. She grinned as she stood over the body with the smoking gun.

The gunfire didn't distract Cartier from continuing to rummage through everything in the bedroom. They had planned on murdering him anyway. Cartier just did the deed a little too soon.

The driver walked into the walk-in closet. "Don't forget about my cut — I'm the one that put y'all on to him and that bitch."

Quinn looked at him and smirked. "We got you." And then she turned the gun on him and fired.

Pop!

The bullet penetrated his skull, and he dropped face-first onto the carpet. The driver was a liability, and they couldn't afford to keep him alive. He knew too much. His betrayal cost him his own life.

"Let's go," Cartier said.

They hurried out the master bedroom and descended down the stairway and out the front door. Quinn climbed behind the wheel of the Benz G-Class SUV, Cartier into the passenger seat, and they sped away with their score for the night.

As they drove back to the Motel 6, Cartier made the phone call.

"Yeah," Mills answered.

"Just do it." Cartier hung up.

Fuck everyone! Yeah, fuck the world! The way Cartier saw it, everyone was responsible for her daughter's kidnapping. And Miami was going to pay and pay dearly with money and lives.

Mills stood up from the bed. He turned to look at Felicia, who was tied naked to the bedpost, her arms and legs outstretched. She was gagged with a washcloth and in despair. He walked up to her with the pistol in his hand.

Felicia squirmed and mumbled something incoherent. As Mills reached closer, tears started to form in her eyes and fall. He gazed at her for a moment. She was such a beautiful woman, but she had to die. She'd seen his face and was a witness to his deadly actions.

He removed a pillow from off the bed and pushed it against her face. She squirmed wildly, but her cries were muffled by the washcloth stuffed in her mouth. She fought hard to free herself, but her restraints were unyielding.

Mills shoved the pillow against her face with strength, then placed the barrel of the 9mm into the pillow and didn't hesitate in squeezing the trigger. The shot was stifled, but the bullet crushed into Felicia's skull, and instantaneously her squirming and grunting ended.

He walked out the room expressionless. It was only business, nothing personal.

CHAPTER 21

Quinn and Cartier had carried out a series of gruesome robberies across Miami in the past forty-eight hours. Their victims were obtuse and much easier to hit up than Domea. A pretty face, a short skirt showing off their toned legs, and a whiff of pussy would lure the dope boys and young ballers, and before they knew what was going on, Quinn or Cartier had a gun to their head and was shouting out orders to them. After they got their prize, they killed them. It was a take-no-prisoners attitude.

It was petty, but everything was turning out to be somewhat profitable. And it was too seducing the crown ballers with their icy jewels who were making it rain in the strip clubs, and bottle-popping with their homies. Cartier and Quinn were the cream of the crop once they strutted into the clubs, grabbing the men's attention without difficulty. The ballers were wearing over a hundred thousand dollars in jewels, but the ladies got only half of that in the black market. They put their lives at risk because time was running out. And it wasn't as risky as going up against a dozen hustlers guarding tons of methamphetamine and bundles of cash.

But their reputation was spreading like wildfire. The game was on alert, and death was knocking on everyone's door. People pointed fingers at each other, stirring up distrust and blame, and lives were being cut down ferociously in Miami, especially after the bodies of Domea, Felicia, and a well-known Miami Gotti Boys hustler were found shot to death.

Cartier didn't think about any of it. She didn't care what was happening in the streets, or who was dying. As long as she was getting that money to bring her daughter back home, it was fuck whoever. And Quinn was right behind her.

The trio lingered around the motel room counting money and appraising jewelry. In two days, they'd robbed and killed three hustlers, two connected to the Miami Gotti Boys and one independent from Little Haiti who was caught slipping when he tried to push up on Cartier at the bar. He was simple to get at. He was willing to follow Cartier anywhere, intoxicated by the prospect of a quick fuck. They snatched his life and sixty thousand from him.

After counting the money on the bed, Cartier huffed with despair. "This ain't enough!"

"We tryin', Cartier." Quinn blew out some cigarette smoke.

At the end of the day, the trio had only raised six hundred and eighty thousand dollars, with the bulk of the ransom coming from Domea. They were still short. And with two days left, it was becoming scary.

Mills sat by the table inspecting his guns once again, while Cartier was trying to brainstorm their next score, stress written heavily across her face. Once again, the girls went without much sleep, and every day was a risk.

Cartier's cell phone rang. She knew it had to be the kidnappers. She snatched the phone from off the bed and answered. "Yes!"

"You've been a really busy bitch," the distorted voice said.

"Where is my daughter? I want to talk to her," she hollered.

"She's still in good hands—for now, anyway."

"Put her on the phone!"

"This was just a courtesy call. I see you have Miami running red with blood. Maybe we underestimated you. Too bad you're not playing on our end; it would have been nice. Forty-eight hours, Cartier, forty-eight hours. And after that, this little game between us will finally come to an end. How will it end? Well, that's up to you. But it's been fun."

The call went dead, leaving Cartier fuming. They were taunting her. She felt like a squashed bug under someone's shoe.

Cartier tossed her phone and screamed at the top of her lungs. She was tired of everything. She smashed the window into pieces and tore the bed apart. She needed to release the pent-up frustration and anger inside of her. She started to cry. She felt so helpless. No matter what she thought of and executed, it still wasn't enough. But she couldn't lose her daughter, not now. She had come too close.

Cartier was on the floor with her back against the wall, looking defeated, when an idea suddenly came to her. Drying her tears, she looked up at Quinn.

The only place where they could get a large amount of cash within minutes was a bank. Cartier had to do it. On any given day, a bank vault and the tellers held close to a quarter of a million or more.

"We gotta rob a bank," she said to them.

"Whaaat?" Quinn dragged out the question but she was in disbelief.

"It's the only way."

"That takes time and planning, Cartier," Mills chimed.

"Fuck that! We can do this. And we don't have time."

Quinn and Mills looked reluctant. They had less than forty-eight hours to scope out a bank and methodically plan the robbery. It seemed impossible. But Cartier had pulled off the impossible in several days, so this would be just another obstacle to overcome. And at nights they were going to still hit the clubs and set up the dealers and the ballers. The walls were closing in on Cartier, but she was determined to keep them up for as long as she could.

Bones stood over the body in the city morgue, the room quiet and still with death. His mood saddened, and his face was menacing, but the tears didn't fall. They'd stopped falling long ago.

Death wasn't new to Bones. He had grown up around it, witnessed it numerous times, and had made it happen to others himself when he squeezed with his trigger finger. But now death had reached close to home once again — first, his cousin Rico, and now Rustic, a childhood friend he considered a brother. He sighed heavily, staring at his homeboy sprawled out on the morgue slab naked. The bullet had torn though his heart.

The mortician stood close by the gangbanger silently, giving Bones some time to grieve inwardly for his friend.

The sudden war with the Ghost Ridas in Miami was coming at a heavy cost. Rustic was caught with a bitch — Domea's wife. Rustic had always been a smooth, pretty boy, dipping his dick into bitches that could get him caught up. And it would have been a major fuckin' problem, because Domea was their cocaine and marijuana connect, but he was dead too. So that problem had canceled itself out.

Domea and Rustic were serious and deadly men, but somehow they had been caught slipping and easily toe-tagged.

"Cover him up," Bones instructed the mortician.

The man nodded and threw the sheet over Bones' friend.

Bones walked out the eerie-feeling room with a heavy heart. He was a marked man and wasn't going to be the next man caught dead. He headed toward the green Durango parked out front, where Shotta was behind the wheel smoking weed. Every step Bones took was careful with his hand close to his .45, which he kept snug in his waistband.

He jumped into the Durango and sat back, his mind spinning with worries. "They fuckin' wit' us, Shotta," he said angrily. "We gon' need a new connect. Fuck me!"

"What you ready to do?"

"Let's go see what Purple and Knotty have for us, and then we could try to get information 'bout what the fuck is happenin'."

Shotta nodded. He started the Durango and drove off back to the hood, skies graying above.

Thirty minutes later, Shotta and Bones entered the one-story home in Little Haiti. Their goons were all over the place, armed with semi-automatic weapons and watching everything from every direction. They couldn't take any chances. They had been hit several times by the Ghost Ridas, and now it was time to hit back.

Bones was greeted by Purple, a lanky, black muthafucka with a blown-out Afro and no facial hair. Purple was shirtless with faded jeans and sneakers, his upper torso swathed in an assortment of tattoos and battle scars that he took pride in. His eyes spoke coldness and death. His knuckles were bloody, indicating he had either just been in a fight or was beating a man.

Bones and Shotta followed Purple into one of the back bedrooms. He had something he wanted them to see. They walked into the bedroom to see the floor covered with plastic from wall to wall, and in front of them were three blindfolded men on their knees in the middle of the room, their hands tied behind them. Two of the men were Ghost Ridas, and the third was Russell, Domea's right-hand man. The two Ghost Ridas had been severely beaten and tortured, but still remained strong and defiant.

Bones walked over to them and stood in front of them. "Remove their blindfolds," he instructed.

The blindfolds were pulled from their eyes, and the first thing they saw was Bones.

"Bones, what the fuck, yo?" Russell cried out.

"Shut the fuck up, Russell! I'll have words wit' you in a minute," Bones replied.

"You dead, *puto*. Ay, Ghost Ridas gon' get in ya ass, muthafucka!" one of the Ghost Ridas boldly shouted. "You dead!"

Bones glared at the young Mexican goon and then reached for the sawed-off shotgun in one of his soldiers' hands. "You talk that shit, muthafucka!" he hissed.

"Fuck you! Ghost Ridas fo' life, *puto*. You dead. Hector and my *chulos* gonna fuck you up."

"Fuck you, and fuck Hector!" Bones shoved the sawed-off shotgun in the man's face, while his men watched on, waiting for the inevitable to happen.

The Mexican gangster stared up at Bones brashly, accepting his fate.

Bones returned the man's unrelenting stare and without any hesitation pulled the trigger.

Boom!

The explosion rocked the room and took the man's head clear off, spraying blood, bones, and brain matter everywhere. His body fell forward at Bones' feet. It was a horrifying sight, but everyone in the room was used to the gory violence. It was their way of life.

Bones stepped over to the next Ghost Rida, the shotgun gripped in his hand. He glared at the man and shouted, "You gonna curse me out too, muthafucka?"

The man glared up at Bones and kept silent.

Bones smirked. He raised the sawed-off shotgun to the man's face and thrust it against his forehead. "Any last words, muthafucka?"

The man's breathing intensified, like he was about to have a panic attack. He scowled and braced himself for death.

There was a dramatic pause, and then the boom came. The loud shotgun blast ripped the man's face clean apart into fragments, and he fell forward against his dead homie. Death stained the room. The Ghost Ridas were now short two thugs.

Bones turned his attention to Russell next.

Russell scowled, his eyes searching for some kind of mercy from Bones. He didn't understand why he was thrown into this situation. Domea was dead, but it wasn't his fault. Bones' fixed stare at him was intimidating; it was one killer eyeing the next.

"Talk to me, Russell," Bones said.

"What the fuck you want from me, Bones?"

"What happened? Why is my fuckin' connect dead?"

"It wasn't my fault, Bones!" Russell growled. "It was these bitches!"

"What bitches?"

"Domea left with these two bitches from the club the other night. They the ones that set him up."

"What?"

"You know how he is when it comes to pussy. I always tried to have his back, warned him about these hoes he be around, but the nigga always thought with his dick."

"Yo, Bones, I've been hearing about this shit in the streets," one of the Miami Gotti Boys stated. "Some hoes out here setting niggas up, gettin' that money, and murderin' muthafuckas."

Bones barked, "Anybody got a fuckin' name on these bitches? Who the fuck are these hoes?"

The room was stumped. No one had any answers for Bones.

"Don't anybody know who these fuckin' bitches is?" Bones looked fiercely at all his soldiers in the room.

Another gang member said, "The only thing I heard — probably like two to four bitches runnin' around Miami doin' that kinda dirt. And I'm thinkin' they might even be responsible for Rico's setup, because one of the cuz out there said he saw some bad-ass bitches lingering around

Rico's that night."

Bones shouted, "So y'all fuckin' tellin' me that some hoes out here are runnin' around rampant in my fuckin' city, fuckin' up my business and killin' my niggas, and don't nobody know shit? That's what the fuck y'all tellin' me?"

"I know what they look like," Russell chimed.

"You do, huh?"

"I'll point these bitches out to you in a fuckin' heartbeat."

Bones stared at Russell, who was now worth more to him alive than dead. "Well, lead the charge then."

CHAPTER 22

The plan was set, and Quinn, Cartier, and Mills were ready to execute it soon. The bank they wanted to rob was U.S. Century Bank on South Dixie Highway, which was out in the open and right near the highway, making it an easy escape. Quinn and Cartier had scoped it out quickly, going inside and looking around subtly.

The place wasn't a fortress. The tellers weren't behind some thick partition, and the open bank vault was in the next room behind them. The bank wasn't crowded at a certain hour, and there weren't any armed guards on the premises.

The girls would do the deed the ski mask way. They would run inside with their guns brandished and quickly take control inside. Quinn would work the customers in the area, making them hug the ground and robbing them, and Cartier would get at the bank tellers and possibly the vault. Mills would be the lookout by the door. It seemed possible to pull off. They were going to execute everything the next afternoon, when more staff would be on their lunch break.

Mills and Cartier were lying up in the motel room chatting, reminiscing about New York. She was talking about her experiences growing up in Brooklyn, and he was telling her about growing up in Harlem.

They started going over the bank robbery. It had to be carried out perfectly. If they were caught, they all were looking at serious federal time, and Christian would be a dead girl.

A quarter after one in the afternoon, Quinn came into the room looking stressed about something. She said to Cartier, "We have a fuckin' problem, ay."

"Like what?"

"We've been fuckin' marked."

"What! By who?"

"Bones an' the Miami Gotti Boys. There's a fuckin' bounty on our fuckin' heads, twenty-five thousand apiece. We made this city hot, Cartier. These niggas are gettin' too suspicious now. If they even smell a setup, it's shoot first, fuck questions."

It was news that Cartier didn't want to hear. But when you play in dirt, you're expected to get dirty, and right now, the ladies felt muddy. But Cartier wasn't going to let a bounty on her head deter her from getting this ransom money and bringing her daughter back home. They had gone through too much to give up now. In fact, it made her even more determined to rob this bank.

"We hit the bank then," Cartier said. "Early tomorrow. We're in and out."

Mills nodded.

Quinn suddenly looked unsure. Her brother and her crew were at war, and she'd been absent from everything for a moment. She didn't want to raise suspicion with Hector, who also had a lot going on.

"We do this and get this over wit', and afterwards, we have to lie low . . . really low," Quinn suggested.

"Once Christian is back wit' me, I'm leaving this fuckin' city."

Cartier had had enough of Miami. She'd made herself a marked woman, and there were too many bad memories for her to stay. First, she wanted to go back to Brooklyn to bury her family, and then it was off to the West Coast to build something new. She would be a new face and have a new identity. There, she planned on permanently burying Cartier Timmons and becoming reborn. The past weeks had drained her, seriously, and there was nothing left.

The flat-screen TV in the room was showing the news, but the volume was on mute. As Cartier and Quinn conversed, something on the television caught Cartier's attention. Breaking news flashed across the screen:

THE BODY OF A SEVEN- TO TEN-YEAR-OLD GIRL WAS FOUND SLAIN, HER BODY BURIED IN SHALLOW GRAVE.

Cartier screamed out, "Turn that up!"

Mills turned the volume up, and the three started to listen and watched as the reporter on scene informed the city of Miami that a young girl was found dead off US 41. Cartier stood frozen to the carpet, her heart in her stomach. The girl they said they found was the same age as Christian. There was an aerial view of the crime scene from the helicopter circling above, and news cameras were everywhere. It looked like a circus.

"It's not her, Cartier," Quinn said.

Cartier remained silent, trying to hold back the tears. Her gut instinct was telling her that it was Christian they'd found. The tears started to fall, trickling down her face like a spring shower. She wanted to wake up from this nightmare. The thought of the girl found being her daughter was troubling.

It suddenly became hard for her to breathe. She stumbled backwards toward the wall, and then her knees buckled. Next thing she knew, she was on the floor. She felt paralyzed. Quinn and Mills rushed over to her aid, but gravity and grief kept her stuck to the floor.

Cartier knew it was Christian they'd found. Everything in her body and soul screamed that her daughter was dead. But how could that be?

Her time hadn't run out yet. *What the fuck is going on? What kind of sick, twisted game are these kidnappers playing?*

In the wee hours of the morning, Cartier and Quinn went down to the city morgue to identify the body. Every step Cartier took inside the morgue was extremely painful and difficult. Her eyes were almost blinded with tears, and her body felt frail. She followed the officers and coroner to the room containing the body. The girl was found by a cleanup crew doing maintenance on the highway. The little girl was naked and badly decomposed.

Cartier and Quinn walked into the dreary, spine-chilling refrigerated room, where there was a small freezer for long-term storage of unclaimed bodies, which were becoming more numerous in Miami. The building held up to seventy corpses, and the room smelled of antiseptic cleaning products, decomposition and death.

The coroner had removed the body from the cot to the morgue table earlier and covered it with a long white sheet. The body had an ID band on the wrist, and a toe tag, and the indentation in the sheet was small, indicating a slight frame on the table.

Cartier felt like she couldn't breathe. She clutched Quinn's hand as the coroner was ready to remove the white sheet that covered the body on the slab. The detective standing behind them nodded, as the coroner slightly pulled back the sheet, revealing the face and neck of the little girl underneath.

Instantaneously, Cartier knew it was Christian. A mother would know her own child, no matter what the body looked like.

She burst out into tears and grief, her chilling cries echoing in the room and blaring throughout the building.

"Oh God! Noooooo!!!" she screamed in agony.

She went to grab for her daughter, yearning to pull her baby girl into her arms and console her, but she was at once held back from doing so. It was still a crime scene, and the body was still evidence.

Cartier dropped to her knees, her body going limp and her tears falling. It was her. The cops had their identification.

The body was covered up once again, and Cartier continued to scream and cry. She was then told that Christian had been dead for roughly two weeks, but the body's decomposition had accelerated due to Miami's exceptionally warm climate. Cartier didn't believe him, because she'd spoken to her daughter only a few days earlier.

"We should go, Cartier." Quinn felt something wasn't right. The way the detectives were gazing at them told her something was about to go down.

But Cartier wasn't in any mood to leave her daughter so suddenly. Even though she was dead, she still yearned to be in the room with her. But the authorities wouldn't allow it. She was dragged outside the room still fighting them and crying out. "I want my baby back! I want her back! Give her to me! Christian! Christian!" she screamed out madly. "This isn't fuckin' happenin'.. No! No! No!"

"Cartier, let's go!" Quinn said sternly.

She had Cartier wrapped into her arms. It was a struggle, but Cartier was finally removed from the room.

Cartier regained her composure, but she was completely torn on the inside. She knew Quinn was right. They had to leave. Her daughter was dead, and somebody had to pay with their life. She wanted Miami to burn and burn like hell fire.

The minute they stepped out of the building, a few detectives and local police were outside waiting to confront them. Cartier recognized Detective Sharp immediately.

"Cartier, we need to have a few words with you down at headquarters," Detective Sharp said.

"For what?" she snapped.

"About your daughter."

Cartier and Quinn found themselves surrounded by Miami-Dade police. Things weren't looking too good. She glared at the detective and asked, "Am I under arrest?"

"We just need for you to come with us for questioning."

Quinn shouted, "Don't y'all have any respect? She just lost her daughter, an' y'all come wit' this bullshit?"

"We just want to ask some questions."

"Questions!" Quinn screamed. "She's fucking grieving here!"

Uniformed officers came in ready to defuse the hostile situation that was escalating in the street.

Cartier felt like she didn't have a choice. Reluctantly she walked away with Detective Sharp and his partner and was escorted into the backseat of an unmarked car.

Quinn was left standing there. It was hopeless to intervene. She couldn't go up against the police. She watched her friend being carted off to jail, she assumed.

An hour later, Cartier sat in the windowless room alone. She wasn't handcuffed, but had been detained in the locked room with the bland décor. She knew she was a suspect. The fact that her daughter had been murdered a week or two ago and she had never reported her missing sounded like another Casey Anthony case all over again. And then the slaughter of her family started to bring up red flags. And the press was all over it.

It was a perpetual nightmare. While Christian was lying in the morgue, she was being detained because they thought she did the unthinkable — murder her own child. It was far from the truth, but would the detectives believe her?

The door to the room opened, and Detectives Sharp and Lam stepped inside. Then another suit-and-tie-wearing man followed them. Sharp and Lam took a seat opposite Cartier, while the third man, with his long, narrow face and steely glare, stood in the corner. They all looked at Cartier like she was already guilty; they just needed to pull a confession from her.

"Y'all need to find out who did this to my baby." The moment the words escaped her lips she began to weep openly. As only a mother could for their only child.

The men weren't in the room to hear her sobs. They wanted the truth and as far as they were concerned, they'd already found the killer. Her.

The coroner's report so far said she'd been suffocated and then shot twice. There weren't any indicators of sexual abuse although she was found naked. The body had also been washed prior to dumping, most likely to get rid of any forensic trace evidence.

Another dead child that was likely murdered by her mother, and in Florida, was bad press. It was a brutal killing, therefore making national news.

"Tell us what happened, Cartier," Lam said. "Talk to us."

She shouted, "What the fuck you mean, what happened? My daughter is dead! And why the fuck am I here? Why the fuck am I here? Why? My daughter's dead —" Cartier started to sob inconsolably.

Sharp handed her some tissue and waited for her to stop crying. He started to read her body language, analyze her facial expression, and all the signs of an upset and distraught mother showed on her face. He knew these weren't crocodile tears; this emotion was for real. However, he felt it was stemming from remorse rather than innocence. If she didn't personally murder her child and siblings, then the remorse could stem from her being the reason they were dead.

Detective Sharp sighed. "What happened, Cartier? You can talk to us."

Cartier dried her tears and gazed at the detectives. She had nothing to say. She just wanted to go home and make arrangements to bury her daughter.

"Look, let's cut the bullshit," Detective Lam shouted. "It's a shitstorm out there, and it's all going to be falling down on you. There's a dead girl found suffocated and shot, and you haven't reported your daughter missing at all! The coroner's report says she's been dead for more than a week. Now from the look of things, that's capital murder, and all fingers point to you. And after this Casey Anthony fiasco, I don't think the jury's gonna be so lenient as to acquit another murderous mother.

"We pulled your colorful record and found out you did some time in New York for manslaughter, so we know we're not looking at 'Susie Homemaker' here. This is a slam-dunk case, Cartier, so make it easier on yourself and tell us what happened. Let's talk — why did you kill your daughter and probably your whole family?"

There was an explosion of anger. "Fuck you! FUCK YOU! I would never hurt her. Never!"

Lam ignored her temper tantrum. "You're a mother. You're supposed to protect your children. If you were being a parent, watching out for your child, she wouldn't be dead now would she?"

Cartier lunged for Detective Lam, but she was quickly restrained by the other two men in the room and pushed back into her seat.

"Sit down and relax, before we throw the cuffs on you!" Sharp yelled.

Cartier was seething. She glared at Detective Lam, wanting to knock his head off for being disrespectful. She dried her tears. She was shutting herself down and no longer going to cooperate with the men. Life no longer mattered to her anymore. Everything had been snatched away from her. She had nothing — no family, no friends — but only misery and pain. Suicide plagued her mind.

Sharp realized they weren't getting anywhere with her by being vulgar and mean. He saw she was about to have nervous breakdown. "Are you thirsty? You want something to drink?"

Cartier didn't respond.

"Mike, get her something to drink from the machine outside," Sharp said to the third man in the room.

Mike didn't look too pleased, but he followed orders and left the room.

When the doors closed behind him, Sharp focused his awareness back on Cartier. He decided to use a different approach. "I know you didn't kill her, Cartier, but somebody did, and we need to know who. These monsters are still out there, and we are here for you," he said sympathetically. "But you know what I think happened . . . my theory about all this? Your daughter was taken — perhaps by a family friend, or boyfriend? Someone you know, and you chose to keep the incident a secret."

"Where are you going with this, Sharp?" Lam asked. "That's Casey Anthony's defense. Why are you trying to give her an out?"

Sharp cut Lam a stern look to silence him. Lam should have known better than to interfere with his line of questioning. To challenge him in front of the perp was undermining Sharp's authority. He went on with, "This person, this monster, took everything from you. Help us help you."

Detective Sharp placed a manila folder in front of Cartier and opened it up. It contained several graphic pictures of Christian, Trina, Prada, and Fendi. He spread them out, so Cartier could get a clear look at each one of them.

"Do you know who did this?" Sharp asked.

Cartier didn't even cringe at the blood-splattered bodies displayed on the glossy photos in front of her. She shook her head no.

Sharp then asked, "Did you do this?"

"I want my lawyer," Cartier replied dryly.

Sharp sighed. He leaned backwards in his seat, knowing once she asked for her lawyer, the interrogation had to stop. They didn't have enough evidence to arrest and indict her. And the GPS he'd placed underneath her vehicle didn't show anything critical to their cases. Most of the time the Range Rover had sat parked in a garage on the outskirts of town. Detective Lam and Sharp looked defeated, but it was far from over. They had the right to detain her for twenty-four hours, after that, if they didn't have anything to charge her with, then she had to be let go. They removed themselves from the chairs and left the room.

"We gonna have to eventually let her go," Sharp said to Lam.

"Let the bird out the cage and she'll fly away."

"Maybe, but if we break her wings she won't be able to fly far."

Twenty-four hours later, Cartier stepped out of the police building a free woman. But she was far from delighted. In the physical, she was free, but inside, she was locked and chained to the pain of losing her daughter and family. She was flanked by her attorney, Jennifer Massenburg, as she descended the stairs and hastily moved toward the idling SUV.

Once she stepped out the gates, cameras started flashing and the screaming journalists swarmed down at her.

"Cartier Timmons-Payne, did you murder your daughter?" one reporter shouted.

"Cartier, tell us what happened to your family."

"Cartier, is it true you were the ring leader of a notorious New York drug crew?"

"Cartier, what brought you down to Miami?"

"Cartier, is it true you are head of the Cartier Cartel?"

Cartier ignored them all, pushing her way through the throng of reporters, and rushed into the backseat of the Escalade. There were too many people everywhere. She couldn't breathe.

Quinn was riding shotgun, and Mills was behind the wheel ready to go.

"Get me the fuck outta here," Cartier said, looking flustered.

Mills nodded and slowly moved his way through the people and traffic.

"We gonna be okay, Cartier," Quinn said. "I got my people an' the streets, an' as soon as they get a whiff of information 'bout any muthafuckas responsible, we gon' be on it. But in the meantime, we all gotta remain low. It's too hot out there for us right now. Hector is becomin' suspicious of everything, we got contracts on our heads, and the police are on us now, so we gotta watch our back. We gotta be careful."

Cartier didn't respond. She sat slumped in the backseat of the SUV with a blank expression, her mind drifting elsewhere. She was dirty, exhausted, and emotionally drained. She felt like dying. But first she had to get her revenge. Her daughter and family's death wouldn't be in vain.

After they made it to the Motel 6 and parked in the back, Quinn decided it was time to check out. Cartier had stayed there too long and needed to relocate.

Cartier remained despondent. Quinn was talking, but she wasn't doing too much listening. She went into the bathroom and locked the door. She stripped from her clothing to take a needed shower.

The water cascaded off Cartier's brown skin. She just wanted to wash away all of her grief. She wanted the miseries and troubles to spill out into the shower drain. She hung her head low and started to cry heavily. Her tears fell like the water from the showerhead above.

Christian was all she could think about. She felt herself drowning in her tears. She fell to her knees and wailed. Where did she go wrong? How did she fuck up? Cartier lingered in the shower for a long moment until the last tear fell.

Cartier exited the bathroom an hour later, her tears dried, her mood desensitized to any more pain. Now it was payback unto those who did her wrong. The first thing she needed to do was call Janet. Quinn handed her the cell phone.

Cartier dialed Janet's number and walked toward the window. She peered out at the sun fading over Miami.

Janet answered, "What the fuck is goin' on down there, Cartier? I heard about Christian. I was just about to call you. It's on the news up here too."

"They killed my baby, Janet. But I'ma kill every last person involved—whoever's behind this. I swear, I'm gonna hunt them down and tear them apart limb from limb."

"Get the fuck outta Miami, Cartier. Come back to New York, and come see me immediately. I have something important to tell you. Something, really important. And stop talking reckless over these phones. You know those peoples could be listening."

It was part of Cartier's plan to leave Miami. She needed to regroup, but she also wanted to wait until the coroner released her daughter's body, and then she would leave on the next thing smoking. She hadn't been officially charged with any of the murders, but the cops were definitely still investigating her, and it probably was only a matter of time until they found some charges to stick to her.

Cartier wanted to take her daughter back to Brooklyn and bury her next to her father.

"Go back to New York an' handle ya business," Quinn said to her. "I'll handle things down here. I promise you, word gon' stay out on da streets 'bout this shit, an' me an' my goons gon' be on the hunt."

Cartier nodded. It was official. She'd be heading back to New York.

❧ CHAPTER 23 ❧

Hector stepped out of the SUV with Tumble by his side, and three scowling thugs following them, watching his back, each man armed with semi-automatic pistols. The fire in the kitchen was getting hot, but Hector and his hoodlums weren't ready to burn anytime soon.

West Little Havana was vibrant under the full moonlight. The people in the streets were joyous and partying like it was New Year's Eve as Little Havana hosted its annual Calle Ocho Street Festival, salsa music blaring in the distance.

Hector walked toward the burgundy Chevy Cruze parked on the street. Three of his peoples were standing by it. The look on their faces already told the horrors they were about to see, and while everyone was carousing and feeling jovial just a few blocks away, the Ghost Ridas had a major crisis to deal with.

Hector walked up to Luis, one of his street lieutenants, and said, "What the fuck is in the trunk, Luis?"

"It ain't pretty," Luis replied with a gloomy stare. He opened the trunk.

Hector stared down at Tosar and Ortiz, wrapped in plastic, their heads blown off. It was a messy sight, but Hector remained expressionless.

Luis said, "Look what these *putos* did to them."

Hector remained silent, his eyes hooked into his two longtime friends who met with a ghastly fate by their enemies' hands.

"I got the call earlier tellin' us where to find their bodies. Bones an' all them *putos* gotta pay for this, yo."

"Shut the fuckin' trunk!" Hector barked.

Luis closed the trunk. "What you ready to do, Hector? This shit wit' the Miami Gotti Boys, it can't go on. It's bad for business. We catchin' heat on this shit. We both know it."

Hector shouted, "You think I don't fuckin' know?"

"I'm just sayin'—"

"Shut the fuck up, Luis! I got this under control."

"I hear you."

Hector stood tall among his soldiers and refused to look exposed and perplexed. Instead he remained pensive. "Clean this shit up," he said to Luis.

Hector and Tumble started to walk back to their SUV. Before they climbed back in, Tumble said to Hector, "What 'bout ya sister?"

"What about her?"

"Word on the street is she's into some serious shit that's spillin' out of control. That thing wit' Cartier, her, and that dead girl, it's gettin' crazy. An' there's a twenty-five-thousand-dollar contract on their heads. Shit is 'bout to hit the fan, Hector. And it's blowin' back on us."

"You get in touch wit' her and tell her to meet wit' me ASAP. Fuck is goin' on wit' her?" Hector growled.

Tumble nodded.

Hector sighed heavily as he got into the vehicle. He wanted to confront Quinn and hear what she had to say. Was she the centerpiece behind this sudden war with the Miami Gotti Boys? If so, then she had to be dealt with. But the war was going to continue, no matter how it started. Both gangs had gone into unforgiving territory, so it didn't matter how it started and why. If it was over a lie, then they were going to continue to fight each other and kill each other over that lie. The Ghost Ridas didn't back down from anyone. And they were going to be heard loud like thunder in the sky. And for that to happen, they needed to re-up on their guns.

As Tumble drove off, Hector got on his cell phone to call his gun connect. The phone rang a few times before Yero answered.

"Yero," Hector greeted.

"My friend Hector, what's the pleasure with this phone call?" Yero said in his distinctive tone.

"We at war, Yero, an' I need a sizeable supply of weaponry from you."

"I see, I see."

"How soon can we link up?"

"In three days, my friend. I have a truckload of some high-end stuff you might be interested in."

"A'ight."

"And I'll give you good deal."

"You know I'm good for it."

"That's why I give you good deal," Yero reiterated.

Hector hung up. He'd made his move on the chessboard, and now it was time to holla, "Checkmate."

Quinn looked like a Hollywood diva as she stepped out of her Escalade onto Washington Avenue in South Beach in her black satin dress. She gazed at Bella Cuba Restaurant for a moment before walking into the pristine place. She was buttonholed by the modern tropical atmosphere and the Cuban classics in the background. Their carefully selected wines and extended cocktail list included authentic Cuban rum like Havana

Club and Matusalem, and from their famous blueberry mojitos to the wide range of fresh Cuban cigars, all this combined to give the restaurant a cozy, intimate feeling.

Quinn was now alone in the city. Cartier and Mills had gone back to New York to handle business. And with a bounty on their heads, it was best for them to split up and lay low.

She looked around the establishment for the man she was meeting with. The spot was brimming with clientele having brunch. She saw him seated in the corner by the window, dining alone. He was dressed casually in a grey single-breasted two-button jacket with side vents in the back, and dark jeans for a fashionable twist. At six-one, he was strikingly handsome with a pencil-thin goatee, had brown skin, and looked somewhat Middle Eastern. He had a rakish smile.

Quinn strutted over in her stylish stilettos and took a seat opposite him. "Yero," she greeted.

Yero was pleased to see her. "Quinn, you look beautiful, like always."

"Thanks. Now where's my money? I told you I would deliver."

Yero's forte was guns. He had them all for sale to the right buyers — AK-47s, pistols, M-16, grenade launchers, Desert Eagles, and remarkably, a few .50-caliber rifles.

He nodded. "Yes, you did. Your brother just put in an order, and I plan to deliver in two days." He pulled out a bulky beige envelope and subtly slid it to Quinn. "Here's your cut — twenty percent, fifty thousand dollars."

Quinn took the cash and smiled. "Always a pleasure doin' business wit' you, Yero."

"It is. You made a war happen between your gang and the Miami Gotti Boys. I had my doubts at first, but you're one smart business woman."

"You sound shocked?"

He chuckled. "Sensitive, huh? But because of you and your friend, lots of violence and murders are happening in this city, many people dead, but my business increases a great deal, because of the war between those two gangs. How do you feel, Quinn, putting your own people in harm's way?"

"It's only business." Quinn tried to use the most generic response to defend her actions. "I just want what's mine. I'm 'bout gettin' paid. Hector got his drugs an' hoes. Me, I'll take the gun business any day."

"Yes, business. And business is good."

"Very good."

"Question for you, Quinn . . ."

"And what's that?"

"Your friend, Cartier. You had a hand in the murdering of her daughter and her family?" he asked. "I mean, is it the reason why you were able to set all of this off?"

Quinn cut her eye at him. "My blood doesn't run that kind of cold. I don't kill kids. I just took advantage of the situation she was in, an' ran wit' it. She's a fuckin' friend, so I appreciate you keep her name out ya mouth an' don't ever repeat what you just said to me about Cartier's daughter to anyone."

"Understandable."

"Anyone!" Quinn stuffed the money into her bag and stood up. Her business was done there. Her arrangement with Yero was a cut from the profits of the guns he sold to the gang members in Miami.

"I see this is going to be a great marriage between us, my friend," Yero said.

"Till death do us part, right?"

Yero smiled. "Something like that."

Quinn made her exit and walked back to her Escalade. She climbed behind the wheel and lingered there for a moment. She thought about her brother. She knew the consequences would be dire if the truth ever came out.

❈ CHAPTER 24 ❈

BROOKLYN, NEW YORK

The smell of Brooklyn reminded Cartier of old times, but she didn't have time to start feeling nostalgic or to reminisce. Her future was bleak and painful, and the only reason she was back in Brooklyn was to bury her daughter. The only family she had left was Janet and Jason Jr., her dead husband's son. She thanked God he wasn't in Miami too, because he wanted to stay with his grandmother, Janet.

Cartier, armed with a 9mm underneath the driver's seat, cruised around Brooklyn in a Cadillac XTS with New Jersey plates, the windows slightly tinted. In her mind, someone close had to have given her and her family up. How else did they know where and how to strike? Everything she loved and cherished was taken away. She was ready to go into seclusion or drive off somewhere far and never be seen again, but there was so much that needed to be done. The funeral arrangements had been thought out, and she wanted to give her daughter a huge sendoff/home-going. She deserved a proper burial, and her first priority was to do that.

Next she was to continue being that cold bitch and start doing some investigation of her own and let the bullets start flying. She wasn't going to rest until she was face to face with that ugly fucking voice over the phone, that unforgettable distorted voice that rang hauntingly in her ear. Her daughter's kidnappers had taunted her day in and day out. She wanted to wrap her hands around the person's neck and squeeze until she could see their eyes bulging from its sockets and she felt their soul being ripped from their wretched body.

Her daughter's body was back in Brooklyn, and the morticians were told to take extra care with her. Cartier wanted her to look special and pretty, to go out in style. She had the perfect dress for her to be buried in — a cream lace dress by Chloé.

Even the casket was phenomenal — an antique white 20-gauge steel casket decorated with Disney characters. Christian had loved Mickey Mouse, Minnie Mouse, Goofy, and Donald Duck ever since Cartier had taken her to Disney World. Cartier spared no expense when it came to her funeral, seeing it was the last special thing she could do for her.

At times she would break down into tears with her legs feeling like Jell-o, but she continued on with the arrangements and trying to remain strong. She didn't have Li'l Mama to lean on for support anymore, having left that sheisty bitch to rot in Miami.

Cartier drove around Brooklyn aimlessly. She didn't have a destination in mind. She just needed to think and escape for a moment. The concrete jungle hadn't changed since her departure. It was still the overcrowded, smelly, noisy, gun-toting place with towering project buildings and dilapidated, graffiti-scrawled bodegas nestled on the block. The fellows were out loitering on the corners, gambling and drinking with their sagging jeans and thuggish traits.

She was staying in a rented two-bedroom condo out in Somerset, New Jersey. Cartier didn't want anyone to know she was back in town. Things were too hot, too dangerous, and she hadn't yet unmasked her enemy. So everyone she came in contact with was a potential threat and a suspect behind her family's murder.

She drove to Canarsie Pier and parked. The pier, tucked away at the end of Rockaway Parkway at the Belt Parkway, was a popular destination for fishing and relaxing by the waters of Jamaica Bay. It was surrounded by protected shoreline and salt marshes, the beautiful and natural backdrop making it ideal for picnicking and outdoor recreation. She stepped out her ride and walked toward the railing and peered out at the sea. It seemed easier to just climb over and jump in, but she wasn't ready for suicide. Too much unfinished business.

She gazed up at the crescent moon and became lost by the glare coming from the moon and ocean. This was the place she used to come to when she was young, when she needed an escape from the hood. The water was always soothing and tranquil.

As she leaned against the railing, gazing at the massive sea, she remembered Janet saying to her, while she was in Miami, that she had something really important to tell her. She thought about it heavily. What did Janet have to tell her? Did she know something about her family's killers? She pulled out her cell phone and called her. She needed to know what was so important. She heard the phone ring and ring then go straight to voice mail. She dialed a second time and got the same result.

Cartier didn't have time for delays and decided to just head over there. Janet didn't live too far from the pier. She got back into her Cadillac and hurried toward Janet's project dwelling. After Cartier and Trina moved away, Janet had left Bedford-Stuyvesant and found a less expensive apartment in Brownsville. The memories of staying in the apartment that she'd raised her only daughter Monya in were much too painful for her.

Cartier slowly made her way up the grungy concrete steps and stepped into the narrow hallway that was covered in graffiti and smelled of weed and urine. The floors were littered with empty liquor and beer bottles, hairweave, soiled diapers, and other items discarded by tenants or drug addicts.

Cartier walked down the hallway with her pistol in her hand. She wasn't taking any chances. As she approached Janet's apartment, she could hear a variety of what made the projects the projects — the young mother with three kids yelling at each of them to sit their black asses down; she could smell the strong weed smoke coming from one apartment, the living room full of niggas having an alcohol-and-weed-fueled argument over a Madden game; the blaring rap music coming from another apartment.

She reached Janet's door and knocked a few times, her eyes darting around the hallway as she waited. The pistol was down by her side with her index finger slightly on the trigger. There wasn't any answer. She knocked again, harder this time. It was late, and maybe Janet was sleeping. There wasn't any answer again.

Cartier slowly grabbed the doorknob and twisted. Surprisingly, the door opened. It wasn't like Janet to have her door unlocked. She was old-school and cautious. Something had to be wrong. She walked carefully into the dark, quiet apartment.

"Janet!" she called out.

No answer.

"Janet!" she called out again a little louder.

There still wasn't any answer.

She flipped on the lights and looked around the well-furnished apartment. She moved farther into the apartment, checking the bedrooms with her arm outstretched and the gun in her hand. The bedrooms were clean.

She then strolled toward the bathroom and noticed the door ajar and the lights on. She pushed the door open and discovered why Janet wasn't picking up her phone. She was lying naked in the bathtub filled with water to her chest and bleeding with slit wrists, her left arm dangling out of the tub. And a bloody razor was on the floor. It seemed she had cut her own wrists. Blood had oozed from the deep gash and trickled down the side of the porcelain bathtub and pooled on the white-tiled floor.

"Janet!" Cartier dropped the gun and hurried to aid her friend. The minute she pulled Janet into her arms, she knew she was dead. Rigor mortis had already set in. "Why?" she cried out.

Cartier couldn't believe this was happening yet again. One by one those close to her were being picked off.

Being surrounded by murder, either by her own hands or otherwise, started to take a toll on Cartier. She couldn't be around when the police came. She couldn't be the one that discovered the body. She was already in hot water, and her being there would only add more fuel to the fire.

Cartier picked herself up from the floor and grabbed her gun. She stared at Janet, her eyes becoming watery. Now she would never know what important news Janet had to tell her. Whatever news Janet had uncovered died with her.

Cartier grabbed a bath rag and started to wipe down the doorknob and everything else she'd touched in the apartment. She then made a speedy exit, taking the stairs and hurrying to her car. When she got inside, her heart was beating rapidly, and her palms became clammy. She felt faint.

She started the car and sped away. When she came to the first red light, she slammed the gearshift into park, and thrust the door open. Then she leaned her frame out the ride and threw up onto the street.

She hovered over the pavement for a minute, trying to get herself right. She needed time to think. Murder was coming at her from all angles, it seemed. It had followed her from Miami. She was ready to give up and let it catch her. She fought with herself, feeling her sanity slipping away and yearning for the madness to consume her. There was only so much a bitch like her could take. Once again, was this karma coming back on her for all the dirt she had done when she ran one of the most profitable — and ruthless for her age category — cartels New York had ever seen? She wanted to join her family on the other side but cringed at the thought of putting the gun into her mouth, knowing hell was waiting for her.

Suddenly, she heard a car horn blowing and a man yell out, "Come the fuck on, lady! Let's go!"

Cartier raised herself up and saw that the light had changed to green. She sighed and closed the door. She put the Cadillac back into drive and eased away from the intersection.

Standing out on the private balcony, Cartier was hypnotized by the neighborhood's immense silence. Somerset County was the wealthiest county in New Jersey, and one of the wealthiest in the United States. The area had a diverse landscape and was saturated with pristine homes, soaring trees, and sprawling green lawns and was a blend of urban and suburban neighborhoods, rural countryside, along with beautiful parks, excellent shopping areas, and extensive farmland.

The lavish condo Cartier was staying in was an hour and a half from the city. It was a temporary haven from the hounding of death and her foes. The beautifully furnished three-bedroom condo sat nestled in the quiet countryside within an embankment of trees.

She stood on the balcony in a pair of boy shorts and a T-shirt, feeling saddened under a canopy of stars, her pistol within easy reach. She could never be too careful. She gazed at the countryside looking despondent.

Tonight she didn't want to be alone. She wanted to be held, to be touched and sexed, to feel a brief moment of happiness and bliss, just to close her eyes and be swept away in a sexual storm. She yearned to erase the ache in her body, even if for one night only. So she'd made the phone call hoping he would show up. With Head locked down in state prison, there was only one man she connected with and trusted somewhat.

Cartier heard the doorbell to the condo and went to see if it was him arriving. She opened the door to see Mills standing there unsmiling with his dark eyes fixed on her. She stepped to the side and allowed him inside.

Mills walked into the lush condo. He removed his butter-soft leather jacket and placed it around the back of a chair. Cartier gazed at his chiseled physique wrapped in a snug white T. He had on dark blue jeans and beige Timberland boots, a Glock 17 nestled in his waistband at the small of his back.

"I'm here," he said with a steely glare.

Cartier was ready to collapse into his arms. There was something about him that turned her on greatly. In a way, he reminded her of a younger version of Head with his mannerisms, and even though he was one of Apple's soldiers, he was the right guy to start over with. He didn't take shit from anyone, and that killer nature in him made him the perfect muscle.

She stepped forward with her bare feet against the parquet flooring and placed herself in his arms, looking for some comfort, resting her soft, curvy frame against his chiseled structure. He felt powerful, but warm. Mills unhurriedly lobbed his arms around her and held her closely to his masculine chest. She could feel and hear his heart beating. This stone-cold killer had a heart.

"You okay?"

"I'm not okay," she replied sadly. "I just wanna be held and loved for the night."

Mills squeezed her into his masculine hold. Cartier was ready to release herself to him. She needed this night. She was grateful that he'd come.

"Take me away from here," she said to him.

"Where you wanna go?"

Cartier freed herself from his arms and walked toward the bedroom. The sadness she felt for her family, she'd buried that somewhere deep for the night. She didn't want those feelings to surface again until she got hers.

She was like a crack addict trying to smoke away her troubles. She wanted to travel to a different realm, maybe become lost in some alternative reality.

Mills followed behind her. Once inside the bedroom, he reached for her with his fist clinging to the back of her T-shirt and pulling her back into his arms. Cartier didn't resist. She sprung upward and thrust her lips against his, locking them into a heated kiss. Her breathing was labored, and her chest was heaving up and down, betraying her arousal.

Mills picked Cartier up in his arms like it was nothing, like she belonged to him, and carried her to the bed. She held on tight, her arms wrapped firmly around his neck. It felt like she was floating on air. She wanted to feel protected, and he gave her that security.

He laid her on the bed. He then pulled out the Glock 17 that was stuffed against the small of his back and laid it on the dresser. He stared at her for a brief moment. The attraction for her had always been there, but Miami wasn't the place to advance on it. He removed his shirt over his head, revealing his impressive, chiseled frame with a six-pack.

Cartier removed her clothing and stood stark naked in front of him. She was beautiful and smelled delicious. Mills took in every part of her body, savoring her with his eyes. He stood at the foot of the bed and was ready to climb between her legs. He started his sensual assault on her, but there was no need to rush.

The first sensation Cartier felt was so gentle and so imperceptible. Every touch from him was exhilarating. He kissed on her slowly from the stomach up, moving his hands across her brown curves. The way he kissed her breasts, thighs, neck, and stomach was sending erotic stimuli straight to her clit. Who would have thought that a killer like Mills could be so passionate and invigorating? The way his eyes locked onto hers told her he cared about her a lot — more than he should.

Climbing on the bed, he crawled between Cartier's legs as she spread them. They kissed heavily again, their tongues entwined like vines. She felt exposed and vulnerable, and she was wet like a river. He pressed his body to hers, and Cartier wrapped her legs around him, pulling him closer and tighter. His masculine scent was dizzying.

Mills slid his dick between the folds of her beautiful, bloated, slippery lips, and they both let out a guttural groan. The moisture between her thighs provided the right lubrication. She was ready for him, ready to forget her troubles for one night and fuck her brains out.

She got acclimated to his large size, gripping the sheets and him tightly, using them for leverage. The heat was intense. Mills' lengthy penis size was intoxicating.

As he ground between her legs with rhythm, she groaned, "Ooooh, fuck me! Ooooh, fuck me!"

He pushed her legs back and, inch by inch, dipped his dick deeper into her. She needed this. His strokes were mind-blowing. She dragged her nails down his muscular back and moaned and groaned in his ear, their flesh feeling like it was melting into one. Cartier felt like she couldn't breathe. It felt like Mills was her breath, her life force.

Fully inside her, Mills grunted. Cartier was out of her mind, panting and moaning, feeling that intense penetration into her. He was focused like a laser, grasping her thighs and pounding fervently into her. Mills went primal inside her pussy as their bodies moved in unison. He continued to push her thighs back to her chest and fuck the shit outta her.

Cartier panted loudly and continued clutching the bed sheets, not knowing what to fully do with herself. His dick was really good, and she felt herself on the verge of having a mighty orgasm.

Mills stared deep into her eyes as Cartier held on and met every thrust inside of her. She wanted more. She cried out, "I'm fuckin' comin'!" her nails digging into his back repeatedly, her legs still wrapped around his back.

Their breathing became synchronized, as they both were lost in blissful pleasure. They couldn't fight it any longer, and they came together, crashing into one another, shrouded by a strong lust.

When it was over, Cartier lay spent next to Mills. And for that brief moment, she felt some normalcy. But it was a fleeting feeling.

The pain quickly resurfaced, and the tears started to flow down her cheeks.

Mills looked at her and said, "I got your back. And I'll make it fuckin' right, Cartier. I promise you that."

Cartier didn't respond. She just got out of bed, walked through the living room, and stepped out onto the balcony butt naked. It was out there that she decided to go back to Janet's place and do some snooping around. She felt she was missing something. And it was eating away at her about this secret Janet wanted to tell her before her death.

Mills followed her outside, his dick swinging between his legs like a lead pipe. Cartier glanced at him and wiped away her tears, her eyes pleading for his help.

CHAPTER 25

Cartier stepped out the Cadillac and walked toward the towering project building once again. It was a breezy evening, and the sky was gray and gloomy, the sun nowhere to be found. Cartier could smell rain in the air and didn't want to get caught up in any downpour. Her life felt heavily drenched already. She hurried toward the building and into the lobby.

By this time, Janet's apartment had been locked down and considered a crime scene. The coroner had brought out the body, the apartment had been dusted for fingerprints, and an investigation was fully underway.

Cartier went up to the apartment, but this time the door was locked. She needed access to the apartment. Her gut was telling her there was something inside that she and the police had missed. She figured that a local locksmith could get her in. She drove to Nostrand Avenue to and got the owner of the shop to send one of his employees to her location. The owner scribbled the alias she gave him and address on a piece of paper and told her a service tech would meet her there within an hour. It took more like two.

Cartier watched as the old company vehicle pulled up with JOHNNY'S LOCKSMITH painted on the drivers said door. The older man, with tan leathery skin, climbed out with his tool belt. He was immediately met by Cartier.

She extended her hand, "Hello, I'm Maria Goode. I called about my lock."

"Lewis," he replied and gave a weak smile. His social skills were rusty and almost nonexistent from years of working at a job he hated and was underpaid for. "I'll follow behind you."

Cartier smiled. She spun on her heels and let her ass sway from side to side as she walked toward the stairway, her blue jeans accentuating her thick hips.

As they approached the door, tattered with the yellow police tape and trespassing notice posted over its peephole, his steps slowed up.

Cartier stopped and whispered, "I need my apartment opened. Quickly. No questions. You do this for me and I will make it worth your while."

"Are you crazy?" he asked. His voice rising to an unnatural tone. "I can't get you in there. I'd go to jail."

Cartier pulled him back toward the elevator just in case someone came on the floor while they were negotiating.

"Nobody's going to jail. It won't take you long to get me in and I said that you will be paid, handsomely."

Lewis pulled a worn handkerchief out his back pocket and began wiping his forehead. He knew what she was asking him to do was wrong. "What if someone sees me and calls the police?"

"Do you really think people here make a habit out of calling five-oh? And even if they did, you would be long gone. Look, I wouldn't put you in a bad situation. I swear. I just need to get inside my apartment."

"What happened in there? Why the police lock you out?"

Cartier was becoming impatient. She thought that as soon as she mentioned money he would have jumped at the chance. All this talking — she could have already been inside.

"All that's not important. Either you're gonna help me or not. I can just call someone else."

He thought again. His eyes drifted down the hall toward the door. "How much you talking?"

Cartier had two pockets. Had he made it easier for her she would have gladly offered him five large. Instead, she discounted the price for making her grovel. "Three thousand dollars."

His eyes said what his mouth didn't. He began to dab his forehead and she could see his hands trembling. He looked around again and then said, "I get the money up front."

"Okay, just hurry up. How long will it take you to get in?"

They walked back toward the door as he observed. "Oh this is just a standard deadbolt. Only a couple minutes."

"Well make it happen." Cartier's voice was sterner than it had been the past five minutes. He immediately noticed her mood shift.

"Money first."

Cartier paid him, and within a couple minutes the door popped open. Before Cartier could thank him, he was heading for the elevator. She walked inside and flipped on the lights. The NYPD had already done their job; now it was time to do hers. After completing certain tasks, most officers didn't give the crime scene another thought.

Cartier started to look around the living room for clues about what really happened to Janet. She went into the bedroom and started snooping around. She went into the closet first, looked underneath the bed, and she checked the drawers last.

She went through Janet's drawers methodically, one by one, removing article after article, but she found nothing but clothing, some old documents, perfumes, some junk, and a few pictures. She started going through the pictures. There seemed to be hundreds of them. Some of them were of Janet and Trina back in their heyday, others of Monya and herself. Cartier sat on the bed and looked at each one of them. As she flipped through them, it brought her back to a time when she was surrounded by love and family, when she, Monya, Li'l Mama, Bam, and Shanine ran Brooklyn. And that yearning for more— wanting power, money, and respect—made her form the Cartier Cartel. This was her family, and now she was the last one left. It was tragic.

Cartier remembered how Monya loved the boys, clothes, and money, and how she'd gotten tired of the petty boosting to keep a few dollars in her pockets. She remembered the corner boys on the block who were always hustling their drugs, and how they always flirted with her and her girls. Some boys got lucky and got the cookies though. But as they came up in the drug game, things suddenly changed. And Cartier was doing a lot of crying. If she could do it all over again, would she do it different? There was that perpetual agony rooted inside of her, that reflective feeling. And after she implemented her revenge, what next? She had nothing left, no family, and no friends.

Going through the pictures, Cartier found a few inside an envelope. She removed the six pictures and gazed at them. They were of Janet and some Hispanic male. He was tall and remarkably handsome. Janet was nestled and hugged up against him like they were lovers. And from the background and his khaki jumpsuit, the pictures appeared to have been taken in a prison. Cartier noticed the DOC Sing Sing stamp on the front of his clothing. She had never seen this guy before, and Janet had never mentioned him. She didn't even think Trina knew about him. Who was this mystery man Janet was seeing in Sing Sing prison?

Cartier beyond doubt felt she should find this person. Perhaps Janet confided in him this news. And if not, he deserved to know what had happened to her. She took the pictures. Her next move was to see Head, who was in the same prison the photos were taken in. He had to know who this person was. And if he didn't know, he could surely find out.

Sing Sing Correctional Facility
Ossining, New York

Cartier strutted toward the prison entrance in her conventional attire, wearing denim jeans, a fresh pair of white Nikes and a T-shirt, nothing sexy, tight or too revealing. She already knew Sing Sing's rules and regulations, especially when it came to women's outfits. They had the right to deny and turn anyone away from their visit if they felt their clothing wasn't proper.

Cartier walked behind the stream of ladies, some girlfriends and wives, mothers and sisters to some inmates, and young mothers clutching babies and young children. They were all going into the gateway and moving toward the booking office, which was adjacent to the entrance to the main visit hall.

Sing Sing sat on the scenic banks of the Hudson River, thirty miles north of New York City. As Cartier waited on line, she could see the calm of the Hudson River underneath the morning sun. The glare from the sun on the water was infiltrating the booking office. It was ironic seeing the convergence of nature's beauty and prison confinement.

Cartier stood behind a young mother clutching her two-year-old son. The line was long, and the child seemed restless and moody. Every minute or so he was crying about something. The young mother had the boy perched in her arm and tried disciplining him a few times, but to no avail.

"I wanna go home, Mommy! I wanna go home!" the boy shouted.

The mother and son caught the attention of the correction officers. Cartier remained nonchalant. She eyed the boy and smiled. He flared up in a temper tantrum and started to raise hell for his mother, punching, kicking, and screaming at her.

Now they had everyone's full attention. It was sure denial for them both if the boy didn't behave himself.

The boy's mother looked embarrassed. She yelled, "Stop it, Danny!"

"No!" he screamed. "I wanna go home! Leave me alone! I wanna go home!"

From the corner of her eye, Cartier saw the female correction officer approaching them. Even though the child was young and didn't know better, the inevitable was coming.

The chubby black woman said nicely, "Ma'am, I'm going to have to ask that you and your child step off the line for a moment."

"But I'm here to see his father," the mother returned.

"I understand. But your child is becoming a problem and a safety threat."

"My baby is not a threat. He's just a boy."

The correction officer raised her voice a bit. "Ma'am, this is not an option. We will deny you this visit if you do not cooperate."

The mother huffed and puffed, immediately catching an attitude, and stomped off the line with her screaming boy.

Cartier couldn't help but think it couldn't be her. Christian had been a well-behaved child. It was obvious that Christian was going to be something much more in her life. But that future was gone. Christian was going to be buried tomorrow.

Cartier moved forward and approached the reception desk, where two COs were processing the visitors' information. She gave them her driver's license and provided sufficient information for them prior to her entry. She got nervous every time, because she was an ex-inmate herself, having served a few years upstate for manslaughter. She didn't want to be red-flagged and sent back home. But everything went through okay, and she was allowed to move on.

The main visiting room was inundated with inmates spending time with their family and loved ones. It was loud, but organized and heavily watched by correction officers posted tactically around the square room. The correction officers stood tall and remained keen. Inmates were seated facing the correction officers posted near the entrance, the green khaki prison jumpsuits room singling out the inmates from visitors. Hard-core gangsters and killers displayed pining smiles on their faces as they hugged and kissed their kids and women.

The guard gave Cartier a number and instructed her where to sit. She walked over to the seating arrangement with a short metal table and sat with her back to the guards at the entrance gate. She was nervous about seeing Head. It'd been a long time. Maybe too long. She constantly looked over to where they were escorting additional inmates into the visiting room. They came inside in single file, anticipation displayed on their faces. Black, white, Latino, Asian, it didn't matter; each man showed the same expression once he saw a face or faces he recognized.

A few minutes passed as Cartier waited patiently. She turned to look at the inmate entrance area for the umpteenth time and finally saw Head being escorted inside. She smiled somewhat. Head was the last one on the line. The prison overalls clung to his masculine frame nicely, and for a man in his early forties, he looked good.

One by one, the inmates started to depart from the line and make their way over to their visitors. Head looked around for his visitor. Cartier stood up and waved, and he nodded and walked over. He walked through the room with authority, his tattoos showing from beneath the rolled-up sleeve of his green khaki jumpsuit. Despite the stone and metal surrounding them, he still seemed in control.

Cartier hugged him and gave him a wet kiss. Their affectionate greeting had to be brief though, because there couldn't be any excessive display of affection during visits. It was a blessing and a curse for many of the men — to be able to touch and feel their women, but not intimately.

"Hey, baby," she greeted warmly.

"How you holdin' up?" Cartier knew Head would have gotten the news about Christian.

"I'm burying her tomorrow."

A profound sadness set in Cartier's eyes and in her soul. She was maintaining by a miracle.

Head gazed at Cartier with his cold, black eyes. He saw that she was tired and worn out, but he could still see the determination in her eyes. She would always have his heart. And he wanted nothing more than to be by her side in the streets and to hunt down Christian's and her family's killers.

"Despite everything that's happened, you still look good, baby," Head said with a slight smile.

"Thank you."

"Are you in New York for good?"

"I don't know. There's a bounty on my head back in Miami. I heard twenty-five thousand."

"You stirred up some shit down there. You don't need to go back down there, Cartier. It ain't safe for you anymore in Miami. This is your home and will always be your home."

"And the people that killed my family, I'm supposed to let that go?"

"I'm not sayin' to let it go, but I can't protect you in Miami. I got goons up here that will look out for you no matter what. I'll put you in touch wit' them. You gonna need some muscle. I might be incarcerated, but I still got reach in the streets. And whoever got Scat, I'll find out fo' sure and cut their fuckin' heart out. But you stay ya ass in New York."

Cartier didn't want to hear it. She understood what Head was saying to her, but at this point in her life, she had nothing else to lose, but him probably.

Head reached over and took her hands into his and gazed into her eyes. He wanted to hold her soft manicured hands forever. Her touch brought him back to a warm and stimulating place. He yearned to have so much more from her, but he only had her touch, her fingertips against his. "I miss you, baby."

"I miss you too."

Cartier released her hands from his and went into her pocket. She pulled out the photo of Janet with the unknown Hispanic male. The picture was crimped in the middle. She placed it on the table and asked, "Who is this wit' Janet?"

Head leaned forward and stared at the photo. "I don't know. Why you ask?"

"Janet is dead, but before she died she told me that she had somethin' really important to tell me. I'm thinkin' this person in this photo might know what that was."

"Something about the murders?"

"I don't know. We didn't get that far. There was so much going on in Miami when we spoke that I didn't ask. And whatever it was, she wanted to say it in person and told me not to talk on the phone."

"I'll find out who this muthafucka is. I promise you that."

Cartier nodded.

The two continued to talk until visiting hours came to an end. Cartier stood up, reluctant to go. She gave Head a passionate hug and kiss, and slowly walked toward the area's exit behind the other downhearted ladies and family members, who all expressed grief at leaving their loved ones behind in confinement.

She watched Head disappear back into lockup behind a few other inmates. She held back her tears. Head spent most of his life in prison. He had been one of the biggest drug dealers in New York back in the late Eighties and early Nineties. When his boss Peanut was shot down in Brownsville, Head took over. Now, he was a two-time felon, and one more strike would mean life in prison. Did she really want to fall back in love with someone whose future was so bleak?

Cartier walked out the prison gates and hurried back to her car. Though it was a sun-drenched day, there wasn't anything sunny about her moment. Seeing Head brought back old feelings, and tomorrow she was going to bury her daughter.

Lingering in the car, she held her head low and sighed heavily, and then the tears started to fall. They were always falling. "I can't take this shit anymore," she screamed out.

She reached underneath her seat and pulled out the pistol. There was that urge to put the barrel inside her mouth and squeeze.

It seemed easy enough, but she couldn't do it, and she burst out into a heavy cry.

CHAPTER 26

Head sat in his small cell reading old letters from Cartier. He was stuck in the past and looking forward to creating new memories. No matter what, he realized that when shit got thick, she ran to him. That meant she didn't have any thorough muthafuckas on the outside to hold her down.

It ate him up to see Cartier so torn up inside. He thought about the photo she'd shown him. He leaned back on his cot with the letter in his hands, but his attention was no longer on it. He racked his brain for a solution. He couldn't lose Cartier—not to the streets and not anytime soon.

After she'd left, he immediately made a collect call to one of his sources outside. He put the word out about his boo needing muscle on the streets, and it was quickly implemented. Next was finding out who the man in the photo was. He went to his homeboy Nicky Knots for that. Nicky, a hacker and a con artist, had the ability to get into anyone's business. He was doing five to ten years for hacking and computer crimes, mail and bank fraud, and identity theft. For the right sum, if you needed information about something or anyone, he had the connection outside. Like Head, he kept his ear to the streets.

Nicky was Nigerian and had a bachelor's degree in computer science and business, with a 4.0 GPA. He'd once had a six-figure salary in corporate

America, but became greedy and caught a charge for embezzlement, among other indictments.

Nicky walked into Head's cell. He was black like tar, and lean and thin as a rail, but inmates knew not to fuck with him because he had connections, from the mob to the politicians. It was said he had dirt on everyone in every playing field from the streets and up. It gave him leverage wherever he went.

Head sat up and placed the letter on his cot and stared at Nicky. "What you got for me, Nicky?"

"It ain't pretty. But I reached out to a few people about your girl in Miami, and she's in deep with the wrong people."

"What kind of wrong people?"

Nicky sighed. "The kind that will kill a whole family just for one individual. I'm talking about ruthless muthafuckas known for spraying up blocks with UZIs and burning niggas in tires and oil drums."

"The cartels?" he asked.

"The worst kind too — The Gonzalez Cartel."

Head had heard of them. Hearing that name come from Nicky Knot's mouth put some worry into him. He wished Nicky had said something different. The Gonzalez Cartel was the new power in Mexico. They had over five thousand loyal and deadly soldiers and controlled over forty percent of the drugs smuggled into the States.

"How the fuck did she get into beef with them?"

"It seems they've had a grudge against her for a long while now . . . something about two sisters being killed. And they're out for blood. I'm talking about, from what my sources down in Miami are telling me, they're trying to kill everybody connected to your girl."

"Fuck!" Head slammed his closed fist into his open hand.

"What you ready to do? Because they have reach."

"Fuck 'em! I got reach too. And if it's a war they want, then I'll give these muthafuckas a war."

"Sorry to be the bearer of bad news."

"I just needed to unmask the enemy and see their faces. Now it's my turn to strike."

It was the worst day of Cartier's life. She stood near her daughter's beautifully decorated casket looking distraught, her teary eyes fixed on the burial site. The ground was shallow and dark, and the area around it was covered with an assortment of flowers and pictures of a young princess whose life was brutally snatched away from her. In a moment, Christian was going to be lowered into the cold ground, and the only thing Cartier was going to have left of her was the memories.

There was a deep chill in the air, and the graying sky looked ominous. Cartier stood like a ghost by the grave in a black Badgley Mischka scoop-back dress. She clenched her fists as tears trickled down her face.

A little over two hundred mourners surrounded Christian's casket in the Bronx cemetery. Word had spread throughout Brooklyn about Christian's death, and the community and her many friends came out to say their final goodbyes. She was going to be missed. Apple and Kola stood by her side, devastated and angered by the loss. Teachers from her grade school and young, teary-eyed adolescents from around the way were there to pay their respects. People were outraged by her murder, and they wanted justice. What kind of monster would do such a horrible thing to an angel?

Cartier wanted street justice. She didn't want the law involved. The only thing she saw for these muthafuckas responsible for her daughter's death was endless agony and torture. She wanted these assholes to experience a slow and painful death.

Cartier, Apple, and Kola were flanked by Mills and three of Head's goons. They were her protection, her muscle, and wherever she went, they went. Head insisted on it.

The pastor performing the ceremony recited The Lord's Prayer.

Cartier's tears continued to fall. She held a white rose in her hand, her attention fixed on the casket that was soon to be covered in dirt. The earth was ready to swallow up her little girl.

Mills, standing tall and still like a stone statue, a 9mm concealed under his blazer, continued to play Cartier close. He was quiet and deadpan. He wore street clothes — dark jeans, a black T-shirt, and black Nikes. Mills wasn't the man to dress up in suits. He felt a suit would only slow him down. His relationship with Cartier was going strong. That night he'd spent with her played in his mind like a recurring movie. He also knew about Head, but the man wasn't a threat to him.

The mourners were allowed to say their final goodbyes. Before the casket was to be lowered into the earth, Cartier stepped closer and tossed the white rose on top of it, and others mourners followed her lead. Soon the casket was blanketed by white roses.

She stepped back and watched the caretakers lower Christian into the grave little by little.

"Bye, baby. I'm gonna miss you so much," she said sadly. Her tears ran nonstop.

The mourners started to disperse from the burial site with heavy hearts. Apple and Kola gave their condolences and were both whisked away in dark colored SUVs. But Cartier lingered for a moment. She exhaled noisily then spun on her heels and started to walk away too. Mills and Head's three goons followed her. They trotted across the cemetery, the leaves crackling loudly beneath their shoes, the fall breeze against their skins like a soothing massage.

As Cartier made her way toward the cemetery's exit, she noticed three men in black trench coats moving quickly toward her. They didn't look like mourners to her. She slowed down her walk. Then, suddenly, the flaps of their trench coats were tossed back, and she saw the weapons against their hips — Heckler & Koch MP5. Her eyes widened.

Mills screamed, "Cartier, it's a hit! Get down! Get down!"

The men took aimed and fired. The gunfire was deafening.

Tat! Tat! Tat! Tat! Tat! Tat! Tat! Tat! Tat!

Cartier hit the dirt like she was sliding into home base. Mills took cover next to her, behind a headstone, and returned gunfire.

Two of Head's thugs were already hit multiple times and were sprawled out across the grass. They were already dead. The third thug also took cover behind one of the headstones and opened fire.

Boom! Boom! Boom! Boom!

Bak! Bak! Bak! Bak! Bak! Bak!

But they were outgunned.

The three men rushed forward and were mowing down everything in their sights. Bullets slammed into stone and dirt, and the mourners that were left quickly ran out the cemetery in fear.

Cartier's heart beat like a sprinter. These heavily armed men were relentless.

Mills sprang up and shot back. He hit one, dead in his chest—center mass—and he dropped to the ground, but the other two continued to fire.

The last of Head's goons jumped up from behind the headstone and shot at the last two wildly. "Fuck y'all! Fuck y'all!" he screamed.

The assassins took aim at him and blew him away, the bullets tearing into him like he was paper, eating up his chest and stomach.

Mills saw his opportunity. "Go! Go! Run!" he shouted at Cartier, and she jumped up and took off running like a track star.

When one of the assassins trained his Heckler & Koch at her, Mills fired suddenly. *Boom! Boom! Boom!* Two slugs slammed into the assassin's chest and one into his head. Mills quickly reloaded. Now there was only one.

Cartier was still running, bullets whizzing by her and barely missing her. The last hired gun was giving chase. He was determined to murder this bitch.

Mills gave chase behind him. He wasn't going to let Cartier die.

Cartier saw him coming behind her fast. She ducked behind a large headstone, falling on her hands and knees, and heard shots from his machine gun rip into the headstone she hid behind.

"Fuckin' bitch!" the man shouted.

Mills caught up behind them. The hired gun was so busy going after Cartier, he became unaware of everything else. He was poised with the gun in his hand and shooting away wildly.

Mills rushed behind him and shouted, "Hey, yo!" Before the hired gun could turn around, Mills shot him in the head. The blast scattered his flesh and brains across the grass, and he dropped like a sack of potatoes. "Stupid muthafucka!" he shouted. He stood poised over the body and shot the man five more times, in his neck, chest and dick.

"Cartier, c'mon, let's get the fuck outta here," Mills screamed.

Cartier picked herself up from off the grass, and the two hurried out the place, police sirens blaring in the distance.

Sweaty, dirty, and in shock, she jumped into her Cadillac and started the ignition. Mills was in the passenger seat. Cartier was furious. They had the audacity to shoot up her daughter's funeral. She was so enraged, she ran a red light and almost hit an oncoming car.

Mills suddenly felt weak and injured as he sat slumped in the seat. He looked down and saw the blood forming on his shirt. "Shit," he mumbled. A bullet had torn into his lower abdomen.

"Ohmygod! You're shot!"

"I'm good." Mills grasped his wound, trying to keep the blood from spilling out. "Just drive."

"No. We need to get you to a hospital."

"Just go!"

"No. Fuck that, Mills! You need to get to a hospital." He had saved her life, so now it was time to save his.

Cartier's foot pushed down on the gas, and her XTS accelerated through the busy streets of the Bronx. She was swept away in panic. Today was officially the worst day of her life. The Cadillac zoomed in and out of traffic and rushed through red lights. The nearest hospital was Jacobi Medical Center on Pelham Parkway.

Cartier made it there within minutes. She pulled her car near the emergency room entrance and jumped out the driver's seat, yelling, "I need help! Help me. He's been shot!"

She quickly caught the attention of the medical staff lingering around. They rushed to the car, and Mills fell out onto the pavement bleeding profusely.

"We need a gurney and a crash cart," one of the workers screamed out.

Cartier stood by and watched a half-dozen hospital employees rush to aid Mills with his gunshot wound. Hospital staff brought out a gurney, scooped him up and lifted him onto it, and strapped him down. Then they quickly wheeled him inside the emergency room.

When he was out of her sight, a profound guilt swept over her. She stood near her ride feeling helpless. She felt like poison. Everything she touched was dying.

One of the medical personnel asked, "Ma'am, who is he to you?"

"Huh?"

"We gonna need some information about him and yourself."

"I don't know who he is. I just found him like that, shot and bleeding on the streets, and did him a favor."

"We need for you to come inside."

"I'm not going anywhere." Cartier was becoming agitated.

The female employee was persistent, but she was going up against a slippery brick wall. That climb wasn't happening. Cartier didn't have time to answer questions and be interrogated by the police. It wouldn't take them long to connect Mills to the cemetery shooting, and probably her too.

"I gotta go." Cartier rushed to her car.

"Ma'am, you just can't leave."

"Watch me."

She jumped into her car and sped off, leaving the lady dumbfounded. She raced toward Manhattan with blood on her hands and clothing and Mills' pistol on the floor. Everything was a mess. She was a mess. It happened so fast. Now her family's killers were after her too.

Cartier drove across the George Washington Bridge into New Jersey. She had to get far away from the city. She raced back to Somerset County, the only place she felt safe. Cartier cried during the whole drive. What the fuck was going on?

When she arrived back at the condo, she closed every shade, locked the doors, and went into the master bedroom. She kept a small arsenal of guns in the closet. She removed every last one. They wanted war, so she was going out with a bang.

CHAPTER 27

When Head received the news about the attempt on Cartier's life, he went into a heated rage, tossing items around in his cell block and shouting madly. His eyes burned with revenge, and he wanted nothing more than to break someone's neck. Cartier had barely escaped the murder attempt on her life, and three of his men were dead. The Gonzalez Cartel was going after everyone — man, woman, and child — no matter when or where. Head knew he had to be extra careful. Even though he had influence and power, he was still in a vulnerable place and situation.

The deeper he snooped into the Gonzalez Cartel's business, Janet and her mystery Latino lover, and Cartier, the more information he came up with. Some information was paid for in hard cash or intimidation. The pieces were finally starting to come together. He needed Cartier to visit him. He had finally gotten a name of the man in the picture with Janet — Luis Juarez. He was a member of the Gonzalez Cartel. But there was one problem. Where was Cartier? Since the attempt on her life, she had gone into seclusion. And the people closest to her were dead.

Head was worried as he sat in the prison library with his nose in a law book, but he had no interest in reading it at the moment. He needed to find Cartier.

And then it dawned on him that she might have gone back down to Miami, after he had specifically told her to stay in New York. He was hoping she wasn't that stupid. His brow creased with pressure and anxiety. There was too much going on. Enemies were pouring in on him like a dam had broken, and he felt like the small town in the valley below. This wasn't a time for him to be washed away, though.

As he sat, a familiar face entered the library. The man spotted Head and walked over. He took a seat opposite Head.

"Any word?" Head asked.

"Nah, they lookin' everywhere for her, but she ain't nowhere to be found just yet."

"She's out there somewhere."

"You think she's still in New York?"

"I fuckin' hope so," Head replied.

"What 'bout this thing with the Cartel?"

"I'ma deal wit' it."

"A'ight. I got my peoples in Jersey on the lookout too."

"That's what's up." Head gave the man dap, and the man walked out the library.

Head remained in the library thinking hard about how to get Cartier and himself out of the pits of hell.

Cartier spent several days cooped up in her condo, keeping her movements limited and breaking off all outside contact for the moment. She had to think about some things and remain focused. She was worried about Mills. She didn't know if he was alive or dead. And she knew Head was worried sick about her. There was too much going on—no room to breathe. The walls were closing in around her, so it was time to start building her own structure and leave the one she was under.

She lingered on the balcony. It was a beautiful fall night, but she wasn't living a beautiful life. As the sun disappeared behind the horizon, so did her past life and her sanity. She felt wrapped in a cocoon, transforming. A new Cartier was about to be born. And the one that surfaced wasn't going to be a beautiful, innocent butterfly. Nah, fuck that! She was becoming a praying mantis and was ready to bite the heads off niggas. She had nothing to live for, and every reason to kill for. They had come at her from every angle, killing her loved ones and taking shots at her, and she was still alive, still standing. They had underestimated her, and she was ready to show them that fucking with her was about to become costly.

She had hidden in the shadows of the New Jersey condo long enough. Now it was time to get back out there and make her presence felt. It was time to be reborn into some kind of hellspawn and rain fire on everyone who opposed her. The murder of Christian, Trina, and her two sisters wasn't going to be in vain.

Cartier sat in the main visiting room at Sing Sing with a cold expression waiting patiently for Head to enter. She needed to know if he knew who the mystery man in the photo with Janet was and if he had put a face to her enemies. Her woman's intuition told her Head had put the pieces together. Head always came through for her, so she figured this time it wouldn't be any different.

Head walked into the room looking upset. He glared at Cartier and made his way toward her. He sat opposite her. This time there weren't any hugs or kiss from either one of them or holding hands across the table. Things had changed considerably in a few days.

"I'm glad to see that ya alive," Head said sarcastically.

"Alive and well," she replied coolly.

"Where you been? I had my peoples looking for you all over. You just disappear and had me worried about you."

"No need to worry. I'm a big girl, Head. I can handle my own."

"Yeah, I can see that. But you got problems, Cartier. And your fuckin' problems spilled over into my lane, and now I gotta help and fix this."

"So I take it that you know somethin'."

"The right price, the right people and shit gets said, no matter if you like it or not."

"So what got said?" Cartier locked eyes with him, ready to hear what he had to tell her. Good news or bad, she needed to know right now.

"Your friend Janet, she was sleepin' wit' the enemy. The man in the picture is Luis Juarez. He's a member of the Gonzalez Cartel."

It was news she didn't want to hear. Cartier was familiar with the Gonzalez Cartel. You couldn't be in the game and not know about the Gonzalez Cartel. They were ruthless killers with boatloads of money, and they moved tons of drugs, with influence from coast to coast.

"Are they the ones that killed my daughter and butchered my family?" she asked through clenched teeth.

"I don't put it past them. But you remember Jalissa?"

"What about that bitch?" she growled.

"When you killed them sisters, you triggered a war wit' their fuckin' uncle, Luis Juarez. He's connected big, Cartier, and he's out for blood."

"Fuck him!" she hissed.

Head sighed heavily. "You done opened Pandora's box."

"And I'm supposed to worry 'bout that? They fuck wit' me, and I'll fuck wit' them right back."

Cartier let her emotions overcome her when she'd killed the two sisters. Jalissa was into something that didn't belong to her. That bitch was fucking her husband. She had to die. She disrespected Cartier's family.

And Cartier didn't take any disrespect to her or her family lightly.

"And Janet was fuckin' that nigga?"

"She was into some shit too big for her to see. I never really trusted her, Cartier. I'm sure she told them everything about you."

"Head, you barely knew her." Cartier didn't want to believe it. Janet would never betray her. She was like a second mother to her. "Janet wouldn't do me like that," she argued.

"Think, Cartier. Look at you and her. You and your moms living the life of luxury in Miami, and she's living in the projects. Monya's dead, and you told me yourself she blamed you for that. You think she really forgave you for that?"

"Monya's death wasn't my fault."

"It was, in her eyes. She lost her only daughter because of a nigga you used to fuck."

"We made our own choices, and Monya was a loose fuckin' cannon. Janet knew that about her daughter."

"It don't fuckin' matter. That bitch sold you out."

"And you know this for a fact, Head?"

"Cartier, open ya fuckin' eyes — Janet was hatin' on you."

"So you sayin' she was the one behind all this?"

"She had a hand in it. To what extent, I don't know. Does it matter? Four people are dead because of her—three innocent little girls."

It was still too hard to swallow. But Cartier had learned to never put anything past anyone. She had Li'l Mama killed, assuming she was the one snitching. Now it looked like Janet was the one who'd betrayed her. It was a sickening thought. Li'l Mama was gone because of Janet. If Janet wasn't dead already, she would have definitely slaughtered her and pulled that fuckin' bitch apart limb by limb and slit her throat.

Cartier had no time to linger on regret. "Five."

"Five?"

"Li'l Mama . . ."

Head knew not to pry. He could see the coldness in her eyes. He smirked and said, "So you think you gonna be able to take on the Gonzalez Cartel by yourself? You tryin' to become that kind of crazy?"

"They fucked wit' the wrong bitch, Head."

"Then go and dig yourself an early grave."

Cartier rolled her eyes. She was almost wishing she would die trying to avenge her family's death. It would accomplish two things. Death would put her out of her misery and also validate to her loved ones that she did everything possible she could for revenge. That she gave up everything, most importantly, her life.

"I'll make things right, Head. That's a fuckin' promise. And I gotta do this alone. You've always been here for me, but I can't allow another person to die behind my choices."

He looked at her intently and asked, "How you gonna make things right? You ain't Superwoman. So how?"

"I have a plan."

"A plan, huh?" He chuckled.

"I need you to trust me and not interfere."

"You always had heart, Cartier, and you was always smart, but what you talkin' 'bout right now, it's fuckin' suicide. We at war wit' these muthafuckas. So I suggest you lay low for minute, recoup, and then we think 'bout things. Reach out to these muthafuckas and talk."

"Head, you sound like a fuckin' pussy. When was it they snatched your balls from you and made you their bitch? We never ran or backed down from anyone."

Head was ready to jump over the table and choke the shit out of her. "Bitch, don't forget who the fuck I am!"

"Who are you, Head?"

He frowned.

"'Cuz what they took from me, there's no talkin'. Look at me. You think I give a fuck? Luis and whoever he's connected to, they gonna fuckin' pay and pay in fuckin' blood, down to every last man. They ain't God. They can get touched too!"

"And I'm gonna do that, but not from behind bars, ma. Just let me handle this my way. I swear, I can't lose you."

She remained forbidding and unsmiling. And her heart was ice-cold. "With or without your blessing there ain't no stoppin' me."

"Do you then."

Cartier stood up. It was all she wanted to hear from him. This visit was over. She still had Head's support. He still had an army in the streets, but only if she needed it. Now it was time to reach out to her second party.

❋❋ CHAPTER 28 ❋❋

I t was a cold and windy day, and everyone was feeling the chill in the prison yard, but Head was feeling a different kind of chill. He had no time to relax. Declaring war with the Gonzalez Cartel was suicide, but fuck it, he was ready for any kind of war. The yard was filled with inmates clad in their denim prison yard coats. Whites, blacks, and Latinos were all huddled in their tribal circles while confined within the towering brick walls crowned with razor-sharp barbwire. The guards were perched in soaring watchtowers overlooking everything, and a few other guards were scattered around the yard keeping a cutting eye on everything.

Head took a pull from the cigarette burning between his fingers. He had a lot to think about. Things were tense inside. He had a feeling something was about to jump off. He didn't know with who or when, but he'd been on the streets and inside long enough to know when trouble was brewing. His peoples had fought with everyone behind the walls: Aryan Nation, Bloods, Crips, and the Latin Kings. Every day there was a fight for survival. He had authority, but there was always some muthafucka trying to challenge his power, trying to test him, thinking that time and age had weakened him. But he was always ready to prove them wrong.

Head, being in his early forties, had seen it all. And he didn't come up this far without being smart and ruthless. But today he couldn't escape the uncanny feeling of trepidation.

Dado walked up to him. "Can you buss me down?" he asked, talking about the cigarette.

Head took one last pull and handed him the cigarette.

Dado took a few pulls as the two men stood in silent for a moment. They watched the yard, watched the men scattered around.

Dado and Head, hardcore gangsters from the old school, were the same age. They both had come up in Brooklyn together, and Dado was like a brother to him. The two had caught their indictments around the same time.

Dado exhaled the smoke from his mouth. It was obvious he had something on his mind.

Head picked up on it. "What you need to tell me, Dado?"

"Word around the place is that you tryin' to war wit' the Gonzalez Cartel. You think that's wise?"

"You runnin' this crew now, Dado?"

"No. But you ready to get into some serious shit because of her?"

Head knew he was talking about Cartier. "You tryin' me, Dado?" Head barked.

"I'm just talking, that's all. Four men are already dead because of this shit. And you know niggas is still upset about what happened to Scat."

"You think I don't know that?"

"Jumping into this is bad news, Head."

"They fucked wit' my chick, and now I'm gonna fuck wit' them."

"And how many niggas gonna have to die, Head? Huh?" Dado pleaded. "This is us, in here—our reality! All our lives are at stake!"

Head glared at Dado. "I'm going to ask you this one time. You're either ready to die for me and mines or you're not. Speak your truth."

Dado could no longer look Head in his eyes. "You know I would lay down my life for you."

Head was wise enough to know that there wasn't any validity to his words. Dado had to go. Head was already planning his demise. He would do it tonight at chow.

"You're dismissed, Dado."

Dado hesitated. "Yo, what does that mean?"

"Get the fuck outta my face!"

Dado walked off with uncertainty, leaving Head to think about what had just transpired.

It was time to head back in. One guard remained in the prison yard as everyone moved on.

Head watched everyone as he started to make his way back indoors. He walked behind a few Latino men, their tattoos revealing Latin Kings membership. Two were ahead of him speaking in Spanish and laughing.

The men in front of Head stopped suddenly.

"What the fuck!" Head exclaimed.

The attack came unexpectedly. He felt someone grab him in the chokehold from behind, their powerful forearms crushing into his windpipe. He resisted a great deal; he wasn't going out without a fight. Then he suddenly felt the sharp shank in his back. The blade went through his denim jacket and penetrated his flesh.

Head jerked. "Aaaahhh!" he screamed.

He continued to fight the man off him, but it was useless. He was overpowered. The blade was plunged into Head's back repeatedly, but he refused to go down. The two Latin Kings in front of him then went in for the kill, both extracting their own prison-made shanks and lunging for him.

"Die, muthafucka!" one of them shouted.

The first blow struck him in the stomach, the second strike slammed into his chest, the third in the chest again.

Head felt himself dying, but he continued to fight. His knees were wobbly, but he wasn't going down so easily. He was a strong man. He managed to punch one of his attackers in his face, and then he removed the shank that protruded from his chest and jabbed it into the man behind him that had him in the chokehold.

"Aaaahhh," his foe screamed, releasing his powerful grip on Head.

Even though Head was free from the chokehold, the damage was already done. He stumbled, bleeding profusely from the numerous stab wounds all over his body. He couldn't breathe, and it was painful. His eyes widened with shock when he noticed Dado watching the attack. Then Dado nonchalantly walked into the building. Head also noticed that the prison guard posted outside refused to intervene, indicating it was an orchestrated hit. Someone had to have paid heavily to have him taken out. He dropped to his knees and fell over.

The alarm sounded, and the officers came storming out to the incident. One prisoner lay dead with a shank protruding from his head, and the other was barely alive.

The attempt on Head's life infuriated his men, and a riot jumped off a few hours later. They tossed shit up inside the prison, as they went on a rampage, even going after a few Latin Kings.

❉ CHAPTER 29 ❉

Cartier looked at her new image in the bathroom mirror. She kind of liked it. She had cut off most of her hair and styled it into an asymmetrical blonde bob. She needed the transformation. She lingered on her new look for a moment and nodded. She touched it gently and was ready to move on. This would be her last night in the condo.

The plan was to hook back up with Quinn. But before leaving New York, she had other affairs to take care off. The first thing she did was put her stepson Jason Jr. into boarding school far away from the drama. And she made sure there was enough money in his account to pay for it.

Then she made sure Janet's rotten body was sent off to Potter's Field on Hart Island, a wasteland of unmarked graves for the unidentified and indigent. Cartier wanted to spit on that bitch's grave, but knowing she lay unclaimed in a pine box was almost as gratifying. It was the ultimate hurt though; even family had turned against her. But it was a feeling she couldn't dwell on.

Last, she dropped off seventeen thousand dollars to Li'l Mama's mother so that she could bring her daughter back from Miami and bury her the right way. Her mother, of course blamed Cartier for Li'l Mama's murder, just as Janet had blamed Cartier for Monya's murder. Nevertheless, she took the money.

She also had received the news about Head surviving a brutal attack and being in the infirmary fighting for his life. It saddened Cartier. She wanted to go see him, but that was impossible. Things were heating up and she needed to end the drama.

Cartier carried her things down to the Cadillac parked out front and stuffed everything into the trunk. It was going to be a long drive down to Miami, but worth it, because she had an arsenal in the trunk of her XTS to take with her. It was unsafe for her to travel anywhere without protection, and the airlines left her vulnerable and exposed.

She had made sure that everything traceable to her or incriminating was discarded and destroyed, and had burned papers and other documentation. And she blacked out her past memories, erasing any family from her mind. It was hard, but in order for her to exist, she had to kill her past, permanently trapping herself into darkness. That meant staying away from Head, even though he was in a time of need.

Cartier climbed into her car and started the ignition. There was no more hiding or running. Now it was time to face the problem head on. She drove off and headed to the Bronx.

Confident that with her new look and the dark shades around her eyes that no one would recognize her, Cartier gave the front desk receptionist at Jacobi Medical Center a fraudulent name and made her way to the floor where Mills was recuperating. She heard through Apple that he was alive and in stable condition.

She stepped off the elevator and looked for Room 605. The hallway was flooded with staff and patients, and no one on the sixth floor paid her any attention. Everyone was in their own world, doing their jobs running around, trying to keep some stability.

Cartier always hated hospitals. It brought back the painful memory of watching them pull the plug on her mother and seeing her life fade away. But now wasn't the time to start feeling melancholy.

She walked down the hallway and found the room. She peeked in and saw him lying in bed asleep. He seemed to be in much better shape. His gunshot wound was bandaged, and he had an IV stuck into his arm.

Cartier moved into the room. She didn't want to wake him. She stood a few feet from the bed and watched him sleep. She cared for him deeply, and hated to leave him behind. He had saved her life, came through for her in a dire time. And he was as thorough as they came.

She leaned forward and placed a gentle kiss on his forehead. She lingered by his bedside for a moment. He barely moved. He appeared comatose. She had to forget about him too.

The nurse came in to check up on Mills. She looked at Cartier and asked, "Are you his girlfriend?"

"No. I'm just a friend."

"Oh."

"How is he holding up?"

"He's doing fine. He's a fighter. He'll be able to go home in two days. Will you be picking him up after his discharge?"

"No. He's not my business anymore," Cartier said coolly.

Cartier walked out the room, leaving the nurse looking perplexed. She saw him; he was okay. Now it was time to hit the road for the long drive to Miami.

Cartier exited the hospital, jumped into her Cadillac XTS, checked the clip to her .380, and then got on the I-95 South. It was back to Miami—back to the hell and disaster she'd created with Quinn. She knew it was dangerous for her to return, especially since she'd made a shitload of enemies and ended up with a bounty on her head. But she had a plan, and it was going to work. She was going to will it to work. It was do or die.

But it meant that she would have to throw herself out there, maybe whore herself out to the right man. Either way, she was going to lose herself to the underbelly of South Beach.

After a few stops to get some needed rest, Cartier made it safely to Miami thirty-six hours later. The city was lit up in a hue of colors and was vibrant with traffic and people. And the night was hot.

Her first priority was to get back in contact with Quinn, and then have her arrange a meeting with Hector.

Cartier was exhausted. The drive took a lot out of her. But she continued to push her Cadillac down I-95 until it was about to come to an end, and she exited off the nearest ramp and drove toward the outskirts of the city. She found herself in Homestead, a city nestled between Biscayne National Park to the east and Everglades National Park to the west, and about thirty-five miles southwest of Miami. She didn't want to be anywhere near South Beach at the moment. She'd come down with a bundle of money, the ransom money for her daughter. And she planned on putting it to good use.

Cartier checked into the Knights Inn, a quaint location designed for both business and leisure travel. In the heart of the town, it was the perfect place to lay her head. Not high-end, discreet, no serious traffic, and reasonable. It was critical that no one knew she was back in town.

She strutted to the front entrance, paid for her room in cash, and moved her belongings into the room, which came with a king-size bed, TV, table and chair, and a big bathroom. The simplicity was somewhat refreshing for her, after the hurricane she'd found herself whirling around in.

Cartier sighed as she looked around the room. She tossed her belongings into the corner and inspected the room carefully. Besides the towel rack falling off the wall and a hole by the vent in the ceiling, there was no problem with it.

She laid her guns out on the bed and looked at them: a Glock 17, two 9mms, a .380, and a Ruger SR22.

She shed her clothing, leaving a small trail from the bed to the bathroom door, and stepped into the shower stall. The warm blast from the showerhead above put her in a pleasurable frame of mind. She could feel the dirt and grime departing her body. She lingered underneath the flowing stream for a while.

When she stepped out the shower, she felt new. She toweled off and looked at her image in the mirror. Her new hairdo was working for her. She inspected her lovely curves and smiled. Her body was on point.

She went into the room and donned a T-shirt. Then she started to inspect her guns on the bed, removing the clips from the Glock 17 and the Ruger SR22. For a moment, she thought about Mills. Being with him for the short time he was by her side had taught her a lot. She learned how to clean a gun properly and not have it jam up on you.

Next, Cartier went through her belongings and pulled out the right dress to wear. She didn't have plans to go anywhere tonight, but tomorrow she had to hit the clubs and find Quinn. Her number had been disconnected, and Cartier briefly wondered if she was still alive.

Cartier picked up the remote for the television and clicked it on. The evening news came on right away. The anchorman was talking about a shooting in South Beach.

Cartier changed the channel quickly. Tonight, she didn't want to hear about any violence. She lived it, and she didn't want to watch it on TV. She changed to *Everybody Hates Chris* and sat on the bed, needing to laugh for once, because tomorrow she was going to hit the streets and implement her plan: raise hell for the Gonzalez Cartel and whoever had a hand in massacring her family.

She ended up falling asleep with the remote in one hand and a gun in the other.

Cartier navigated her Cadillac through South Beach. It was full of life like always. In three days, she'd hit up prime locations — B.E.D. on Washington Avenue, and then Buck 15 on Lincoln Road — but it was to no avail. Then it was Cameo, and Club 01 on Ocean Drive, and the same thing. Quinn's residence in Little Havana was cleared out, and there wasn't anywhere else to look but in the clubs.

She'd strutted through the lively clubs cautiously, keeping a keen eye on her surroundings. Changing her look to a blonde bob made her feel a little more at ease, since running into the wrong face at the wrong time could lead to deadly consequences. She came across a few Ghost Ridas partying in the club. She even looked Tumble, Hector's right-hand goon, directly in his face in Club 01, and he didn't have a clue who she was, or was too drunk to tell or to care.

Her fourth night in Miami, Cartier stepped out the XTS clad in a paisley halter minidress with a deep plunging neckline. Her ample cleavage was looking succulent, and the Envy cut-out rhinestone platform heels she wore made her long legs seem to stretch even more.

Cartier walked into Dream, a two-level place with three rooms, 8,500 square feet of seductive French décor, and three extravagant VIP sections. The music was blaring like she was in a concert hall. She strutted through the crowd and walked over to the bar, where she ordered a drink, her eyes scanning every square inch of the place.

And then she spotted Quinn partying in the VIP section with her peoples. She stared at Quinn popping bottles and partying like they didn't raise hell in South Beach robbing and killing a bunch of muthafuckas. But she was under her brother's protection and surrounded heavily by men the size of Arnold Schwarzenegger.

Cartier downed her drink. It would be simple enough to just walk over and make her presence known, but she didn't know what kind of situation she'd be walking into. This wasn't her home, it was Quinn's. And Cartier had started to lose her trust for people. After finding out about Janet's betrayal, loyalty was just a word. It had been weeks since she'd left Miami. Was Quinn still on her team?

Cartier played the bar close and watched Quinn do her thing in the VIP area. She shooed away the thirsty males craving for her attention. Her only agenda was to link up with her friend alone and in private, but her body in that sexy dress kept luring unwanted attention her way.

There were too many faces around Quinn, especially unknown faces. Too risky for a direct approach, so Cartier decided to be patient. She needed to hear the rundown from her friend, what went down during her absence.

The night progressed without incident, and when it was all said and done, she followed Quinn out the nightclub and to her car. Quinn got into a red Ferrari 360 Spider and sped away. Cartier was right behind her.

From the looks of things, it appeared the heat was off her. She was riding solo, no muscle at all, and moving around in style, like she never did.

Quinn drove a few blocks and stopped at a red light.

Cartier knew just how to get her attention. While Quinn sat in her convertible Ferrari idling at the red light, she purposely tapped the back of her, causing the Ferrari to jolt forward just a little.

Quinn cursed loudly, "Muthafucka!" She stormed out her car, ready to make a heated scene. She walked toward Cartier's Cadillac with an angry stare. "Nigga, you can't fuckin' drive? This is a three-hundred-thousand-dollar fuckin' car!" she shouted.

Before she could do anything stupid, Cartier pushed her door open and stepped out.

Quinn stopped in her tracks and looked mystified by the short bob and blonde hair. She squinted her eyes and incredulously called out, "Cartier?"

Cartier smiled.

"Oh shit! Bitch, when did you get back in town?" Quinn asked excitedly.

"Three days ago."

"And look at you — you cut ya fuckin' hair and dyed it blonde. Wow!"

"We need to talk." Cartier didn't have time for the formalities. She wanted information and to move forward with her plan.

"Of course, but not here. Follow me."

Both ladies got back into their cars, and Cartier followed behind Quinn. She had the loaded .380 near her reach and wasn't taking any chances. If anyone flinched wrong, she was blasting them.

The ladies ended up at the Miami Beach Marina. The full moon above and the ocean's glare was a picturesque sight. The deepwater yacht slips were adjacent to the heart of South Beach's Art Deco District. Everything was money out there.

Cartier parked next to Quinn, and they simultaneously exited from their cars. Cartier kept her pistol concealed and close, and eyed Quinn, approaching with a smile.

"Damn, Cartier! You shoulda told me you were back in town."

"I couldn't reach you."

"Yeah, things got crazy out here."

"But I see you coming up. I ain't been gone in no less than a month, and you already pushin' a Ferrari."

"I'm a busy woman, an' made some serious connections," she replied. "But c'mon, we need to talk."

Cartier followed behind Quinn onto the docks where a fleet of yachts and boats sat calmly on the water. The array of vessels was a spectacle of wealth and grandeur. Quinn led Cartier toward a ninety-three-foot Italian luxury yacht. Cartier was impressed. Quinn stepped onto the yacht and Cartier was right behind her.

It was a quiet and cool night aboard the luxurious vessel with three decks. Azure lighting all through the boat tastefully brought to life the cream and sand tones, as well as accentuated the dark tones. The top-level industrially designed furniture and the interior ambiance, created a comfortable, pleasurable place to be.

Quinn had definitely stepped her game up.

"Nice," Cartier said.

"It is, right?"

"How did you make this happen?"

"I'm in bed wit' the right people."

Cartier looked at her friend with suspicion.

Quinn quickly picked up on the foul look aimed at her. "What? You don't trust me now?"

"A lot done changed, Quinn. People that I thought had my back didn't."

"Well, I got your back until I don't. That's the way it goes down in the hood."

Cartier understood. Loyalty could be bought for a price, traded in and exchanged. That was real talk.

"You want a drink?"

"Nah, I'm good."

"A'ight."

Quinn moved around the yacht like a queen. She went over to the minibar and poured herself a drink. She downed it and poured another one. She locked eyes with Cartier. She eyed Cartier's new look and she liked it.

"I need to get in contact wit' your brother," Cartier said.

"And for what reason?"

"Business."

"What kind of business you need to have wit' him? You never had any interest wit' my brother before."

"Let's just say I have somethin' in mind."

"Well, me an' my brother are kind of at odds right now, more like a civil war."

"About what?"

"We see things different fo' the moment. And what do you need from him that you can't get from me?"

Cartier wasn't ready to tell Quinn anything. The people in her old circle were not to be trusted anymore.

"I see, you really don't trust me anymore. Ya hurtin' my feelings, Cartier."

"I been through a lot, Quinn."

"I know, an' I told you I will always have ya back."

"Do you?"

"What you implying?"

"You living lavish all of a sudden — Ferrari and yacht and whatnot — where all this come from so suddenly?"

"I told you, I get mines an' I made some connections out there."

"And what about the bounties on our heads?"

"Muthafuckas ain't gon' touch me. We still at war wit' the Miami Gotti Boys and Bones, but let's just say, I made some influences of my own."

Cartier still had her doubts.

"Look at you, I see it in ya eyes, Cartier. You gotta let that distrustful shit go. In life you gotta trust somebody."

"I use to give my trust away upfront. Now people gonna have to earn it."

Quinn chuckled.

"I think my days of trying to prove myself to you are over." Quinn wasn't in the mood for Cartier's paranoia. Life was too good for her now and she had done more for Cartier than any other person walking the earth. "But as I promised, I wasn't gon' give up until I found out somethin' 'bout who snatched Christian."

She suddenly had Cartier's full attention.

"The peoples I fuck wit' now, they got my back. I'm pullin' in a lot of money fo' them so they look out. But to make a long story short, I got a name fo' you."

"Who?"

Quinn smiled glibly. "Some muthafucka named Luis Juarez."

Hearing that name made Cartier's eyes gleam. Her sour mood against Quinn suddenly changed. It was the same name Head had given her.

"By the look on ya face, I take it that you heard the name before."

"Back in New York."

"I got somethin' better fo' you than just a name — I have an address fo' him."

Cartier was ready to run over there and fuck his shit up. She wanted to thank Quinn.

"You trust me now?" Quinn asked.

"Let's just find this muthafucka first."

"Fine by me."

The two left the yacht and walked back to their cars. Cartier was about to jump into her ride, but Quinn stopped her, saying, "Just ride wit' me. We still need to catch up."

Cartier looked at the red Ferrari, hesitated momentarily, and then decided it was for the best. She climbed into the passenger seat and stretched out her long legs.

Quinn started the engine, and it roared like a lion. Cartier felt the horsepower beneath the chariot. Quinn backed up with her hand on the gearshift and maneuvered out of the marina with ease. She then put her heels to the accelerator and sped off like a thoroughbred running in the open fields.

It was a beautiful thing to see — two stunning women in a thunderous piece of beauty.

The ladies ended up parked outside a towering housing complex on Collins Avenue and 71st Street. The sun was trying to steal the skies once more as dawn gradually came about, bringing a new day to the city.

Cartier sat patiently with Quinn. "What are we here for?" she asked.

"Just wait," she replied coolly. "I got somethin' to show you."

An hour had passed. Cartier had better things to do. She smoked a cigarette and looked up at the sky. She swiftly turned to look at Quinn and asked, "How you know 'bout this muthafucka anyway? He the one that killed Christian and my family?"

"He had a hand in it. And I got peoples lookin' out. But this muthafucka is bad news, Cartier. He runs wit' the Gonzalez Cartel. He moves money and people."

"People?" Cartier was puzzled.

"Human trafficking. An' I'm thinkin' they played us fo' fools. It wasn't about the ransom, I think."

"Then what was it about?"

"I'm not sure. But I'm thinkin' you rubbed these muthafuckas the wrong way somehow."

Cartier knew it was over the sisters she'd murdered in New York. But she planned to keep that to herself at the moment.

"I'm in the gun business."

"Guns?"

"It's profitable. Niggas killing each other in Miami every day. I just help supply them the means to do so. And the shit we done started, I

241

just turned a curse into a blessing. Shit! One man's trash is this bitch's treasures," Quinn said with a sly smile.

Cartier didn't care what Quinn did. She just wanted revenge for her family.

"But the pipeline I'm in, they got significant resources, an' your daughter's death made headlines everywhere, and you know some muthafuckas just don't know how to shut the fuck up. People say somethin', let it slip, information gets paid for, an' I got the word on Luis through a friend who owed me a favor, knowin' I was tight wit' you. I tried to reach you, but you disconnected your Miami cell and I had no number for you back in New York.

"So I just sat on it until you returned. I knew you were comin' back down. I never doubted you once. You needed to finish what you started."

"Damn right." Cartier said with conviction.

A cocaine-colored Bentley drove by the girls as they were seated in the Ferrari. It came to a stop in front the lavish housing complex they were staking out. Cartier watched it park five cars down from them.

Quinn nodded toward the Bentley. "That's him."

Cartier watched the vehicle like a hawk. The driver and passenger doors opened up, and two figures stepped out, one man and one woman. They were all smiles and laughing. Cartier frowned at the dead man walking. He was tall and handsome with dark curly hair and a thick goatee. His black slacks and silk gray shirt hugged his physically fit body. He had a power about him as he walked with a leggy, blonde bitch wearing a microfiber contrast halter dress. She was bubbly and flirtatious.

Luis wrapped his arm around her slim waist and then slid his hand down to her protruding backside and squeezed her butt gently. They headed toward the building.

Cartier cocked back her pistol and rushed out the car. Her family was dead and he had the audacity to be laughing and having a good time. Like her daughter and her family was some measly insects that you squash on the wall and don't thinking nothing about it.

"Cartier, wait!" Quinn called out.

"I'ma kill this bastard."

There was no talking her out of it.

Cartier strutted in her heels with the gun by her side and her eyes fixated on Luis Juarez. He wouldn't even see it coming.

Quinn rushed out the car too. She had a 9mm and her bag in her hands and moved behind Cartier.

Luis walked into the building and got on the elevator with his beautiful date. Cartier and Quinn were right behind him. But they were too late. The elevator had already ascended. Cartier couldn't miss her shot.

"What floor? What fuckin' apartment, Quinn?" Cartier shouted.

"He's on twelve."

Cartier pushed for the call button to the lift. She was becoming impatient. She was itching to murder this muthafucka. Her face was twisted into an ugly scowl, and she couldn't stop her hand from trembling.

When the doors finally opened, Cartier damn near leaped inside and rapidly pushed for twelve. She took a deep breath.

"How we gonna do this?" Quinn asked.

Cartier had no idea. It was one of those spontaneous fuck-it moments. But she refused to let this opening fade from her.

As the elevator was coming to their floor, Quinn removed the silencer from her bag and started to twist on the silencer to her 9mm. She said to Cartier, "Stop bein' so fuckin' impulsive an' think rational. You shoot that off in this building, wit' these hallways n' it's gonna let out a loud noise. And, bad enough, we on like twenty fuckin' security cameras. But I'ma handle that."

Cartier wasn't really listening. The only thing she had on her mind was Luis. The doors opened, and they stepped out into the carpeted hallway.

"Apartment 1208," Quinn said.

Cartier stormed toward that way. Once again, she was back into the life of killing.

They approached Apartment 1208. It seemed quiet on the other side of the door. Quinn and Cartier looked at each other. It was now or never.

Cartier knocked, while Quinn stayed out of view. She waited for him to respond. She stood at Luis' door looking like a pinup diva, her legs gleaming, cleavage showing, and a seductive smile on her lips. She didn't know how this would go, but she had to take this chance. He was alone with company and no muscle around him.

"Who the fuck is it?" she heard him shout without opening the door.

It was a tense moment. Both girls knew Luis Juarez was just as dangerous as they were. One mistake could cost them their lives.

Cartier had to come up with something believable for him to open his door. "You called for an escort, right?" Cartier replied. "I'm Xena."

"What?"

"I'm from Midnight Escort Service."

"I ain't call for no fuckin' escort service."

"Well, somebody did. Got this address and apartment number, and I ain't leaving until this shit gets figured out. I'm out of twenty-five dollars for cab fare here," Cartier said convincingly.

The door swung open, and Luis, gripping a .45, glared at Cartier. He was shirtless, showing off the ripples in his stomach. But one look at her and he went, "Damn!"

"Hey, baby. You sure you ain't call for a date? 'Cuz, as fine as you are, I can give you a discount."

"I ain't ever paid for pussy in my life —"

Before Luis could finish his sentence, Quinn sprang into his view with the pistol aimed at him and fired. *Poot!*

The bullet tore though his kneecap, and Luis dropped back, staggering.

He tried to raise his gun to fire back, but Quinn hit him again in the second kneecap, and he was completely crippled.

"Fuckin' bitch!" he screamed.

The blonde bimbo in the room screamed out, but Quinn silenced her up with a gunshot through her skull. She crashed against the couch and lay slumped over.

Cartier shut the door behind her. It was time for the fun to begin.

The girls moved together like lightning. Luis didn't even know what hit him.

"You know who the fuck I am?" he shouted.

Cartier glared at him. She so badly wanted to shove the heel of her shoe into his skull and twist, but she needed him alive for the moment. She needed information.

They stood over him and watched him squirm in agony. He clutched his knees and was bleeding profusely.

"Who the fuck sent you?" Cartier shouted.

"Fuck you, bitch!"

Quinn shot him again in the leg.

Luis screamed, and Cartier turned up the stereo in the room to drown him out.

"We can do this all day." Quinn aimed the pistol at his dick.

Luis looked horrified. "No, just relax . . . relax!"

"I wanna know — who else was involved wit' my family's murder? I want fuckin' names and locations," Cartier stated.

"You kill my two nieces in New York and talk this shit about retribution! How does it feel, Cartier, to lose someone you loved dearly?" Luis taunted.

Quinn fired.

Poot! The bullet ripped through his inner thigh.

Luis screamed again. He wriggled against the floor in pain. It was obvious that these bitches weren't playing around with him. He breathed harder and felt weak, feeling the blood leaving his body.

"Who fuckin' else?" Cartier screamed. She could feel the tears welling up in her eyes as she thought about her daughter. The things they probably did to her. She knew her baby was scared.

Quinn stepped closer to him and crouched down. She put the tip of the silencer to his balls and ground the barrel it into his genitals.

Luis groaned, helpless and in pain.

Quinn told him, "Tell her what she needs to hear, and I promise to make the pain go away. Or else I'll become a surgeon in this muthafucka. An' I ain't got stable fuckin' hands."

"Talk to me!" Cartier screamed.

"How's Janet doing these days?" Luis taunted, looking up at Cartier.

Quinn fired. *Poot!* This time the shot nicked his nut sack.

"You think we fuckin' playin' wit' you!" Quinn shouted.

The pain was excruciating. "Okay, okay!" Luis cried out.

Cartier was ready to hear what he had to say.

"Janet slowly lost her mind over her daughter," he said. "She always felt you were the reason behind her daughter's death. You and your mother run off to Miami, my city, with a fortune, and leave her out in the cold. I just took advantage of that bitch, made her feel loved, dicked her down when I got out of Sing Sing. Bitch was weak. She gave you up for greed, bitch. But when she found out what we did to your family, she tripped out over that shit and didn't know what our true intentions were. We lied to her, promised not to harm your mother or anyone else. We played you, bitch. I just wanted to fuck with your head and take from you what you did to me with Jalissa and Marisol. You were supposed to drop the second ransom off, and your daughter wasn't supposed to be found not at all, but someone fucked up. And what you was listening to was only a recording of your daughter's voice — that bitch been dead."

Cartier was in full-blown tears. She wanted to fall out in grief from what she was hearing. But she held herself steady. "Who else was involved?"

"You ready to war with the Gonzalez Cartel? Because this doesn't fuckin' end with me, you dumb bitch!"

Cartier stared angrily at him. Her heart felt like it was about to rip from her chest. She snatched the gun from Quinn's hands, and shouted, "Fuck you!"

Luis looked up at impending death and smirked.

Cartier fired five shots into him. *Poot! Poot! Poot! Poot! Poot!* She stood over Luis Juarez with the smoking gun in her hand and frowned.

"There ain't no turning back now, Cartier," Quinn said.

Cartier didn't plan to turn back. She was ready to root herself into the pits of hell. She had nothing else to lose. Her soul had been ruptured from her body, and her heart grew ice-cold. The only thing left to immerse herself into was the underworld of Miami. But she still wanted to meet with Hector. He was still part of her plan.

Quinn made a phone call and informed someone of their situation. She needed a cleaner. Things had gotten sloppy, and Luis Juarez and his female friend needed to vanish. And the security footage of them entering the building and elsewhere had to be destroyed. It was the only thing that linked them to the crime.

Cartier got back into Quinn's Ferrari. She shut the door, leaned back and released a heavy sigh. It finally felt like a huge burden was lifted from her shoulders. She got one of those muthafuckas. She was finally able to deal out some street justice for her family, and it was somewhat refreshing. Luis Juarez had died in agony, and it was somewhat satisfying.

She was ready to let the Gonzalez Cartel and everyone associated with them know that they fucked with the wrong bitch. Miami was home now, like she planned it to be when she'd moved her family down a few months ago, thinking she was going to retire from the game, when somehow destiny or doom pulled her back in.

And her next time out of the game was probably in a box. But she would postpone that fate as long as she could.

❦ CHAPTER 30 ❦

Cartier slept for hours in the king-size bed. It was morning, but the room was dark with the shades drawn. It was the first decent sleep she'd had in weeks. Killing that fool Luis relieved her of a lot of stress, but it only took away a fraction of her problems. Now she had to worry about retaliation from not just the Gonzalez Cartel, but the other fools she'd wronged in Miami. Her enemies were in droves, and without the right protection, she was already dead.

She decided to crash at Quinn's new place in downtown Miami, a three-bedroom suite in a luxurious fifteen-story complex. Like the Jefferson's, she was moving on up. From every room she had a breathtaking view of South Beach, the beaches, and the deep blue sea, which stretched endlessly. It was a slice of heaven for the moment.

Cartier woke up to the afternoon sun trying to infiltrate its way through the shades. She stirred around the bed naked for a moment, stretching, and then realized she wasn't alone.

"Oh shit!" Cartier hollered.

Unsmiling and cool, Hector and Tumble were standing at the edge of the bed looking at her.

Cartier quickly covered her breasts with the sheet and jumped back against the headboard. She had never been so startled. "What the fuck are you doin' in here, Hector?" she screamed out.

"Hurry up and get dressed then meet me in the next room," Hector said in a civil tone.

He and Tumble made their exit, leaving her confused and worried at the same time. She tossed the sheets off her and jumped out the bed. She slammed the bedroom door shut and took a deep breath. She wanted to meet with Hector, but not like this. It was so sudden and scary for her.

Cartier stepped back into the same dress she'd worn the night before, gathered her things, and met with Hector in the living room. He was seated and waiting patiently, while Tumble stood by the floor-to-ceiling windows gazing at a bright and sunny Miami.

"Nice view," Tumble said.

"Where's Quinn?"

"She's not here for the moment," Hector replied.

"What's goin' on here?"

"I need you to come and take a ride wit' me," he suggested.

Hector stood up and smoothed the small wrinkles in his jacket. He looked suave in his custom-tailored, dark gray pinstripe Armani suit and wing-tip alligator shoes.

Cartier looked at him. He was handsome and dapper. A gangster and a gentleman he appeared to be. "Where are you takin' me?" she asked.

"Just shut up and ride with us," he said, a little stern.

Cartier didn't have a choice. She was alone and had no idea where Quinn was. She felt Hector might have done something terrible to his own sister.

Hector started toward the door, and Tumble was right behind him.

Cartier lingered in the living room for a short moment but decided to walk out too. They took the elevator silently down to the lobby and exited into the street. Cartier tried to remain calm, but the thought of karma coming back to fuck her up was milling inside her head.

Hector walked toward a white stretch limousine parked outside. The chauffeur jumped out and hurried to open the door, and he and Tumble climbed inside. Cartier was right behind them.

She sat against the plush black leather silently, while Hector lit a cigar and exchanged words with Tumble.

They rode through downtown Miami for a while. Hector was on the phone discussing business.

Tumble couldn't keep his eyes off Cartier. He was truly creeping her out.

Cartier sighed and rolled her eyes.

While Hector was discussing business on his cell phone, he looked at Cartier and smiled.

When the limo pulled to the side and stopped at the curb. Hector looked at Tumble and nodded. "Take care of that for me, Tumble."

"I got you," Tumble replied. He climbed out the limo and shut the door, leaving Cartier alone with Hector.

The limo pulled away from the curb, and silence overcame them again. She gazed out the window, a feeling of trepidation swimming inside of her. She remained cool and aloof.

Finally, Hector ended his conversation and focused his attention on Cartier. "Heard you was lookin' for me," he said.

"I was."

"In actuality, I should be the one lookin' for you. You and my sister caused some shit in this city . . . a lot of lives and money lost because of y'all bitches. You think I wouldn't fuckin' find out 'bout y'all?" Hector barked.

"They took everythin' from me, Hector."

"And? You fucked up, an' you fucked up huge. You shoulda came to me from the start. Now wit' this shit wit' the Miami Gotti Boys and now the Gonzalez Cartel, I'm ready to throw you to the fuckin' wolves."

"And then what?" she retorted boldly.

"I'll tell you what. How 'bout I watch them cut you into little pieces an' throw your pretty ass in the sea? That's *then what*."

"You think I'm afraid to die?" she said, defiantly.

"Stop thinking you're a tough guy, Cartier. You was just sleepin' like a baby up in that room. That wasn't the sleep of someone ready for it to all end."

Cartier couldn't argue with his logic, so she switched gears. "If you've already made up your mind to toss me to the wolves, then there isn't anything I can say to change that. But I will say that I can be a better asset to you alive than dead."

"And how the fuck is that, Cartier?"

"I'll be indebted to you. I'm smart and ruthless, and I have nothin' left. My family's dead, and New York is now a memory for me. All I have is this rage inside of me. Take advantage of it, Hector. Let me come up under you, become a member of ya crew, and I'll never let you down," she pleaded softly.

Hector chuckled. "You, become a fuckin' member?"

"Why not? Look at what I'm capable of."

"And then I'll have the Gonzalez Cartel gunning for my peoples too 'cuz of you."

"Look at you, Hector. You're a damn king of this city. We can make your enemies tremble when we get done wit' them."

She moved closer to Hector and placed her hand on his lap. She looked at him, her eyes revealing her availability to him. Her touch against him became enticing. "I can be yours, however you want me."

Hector gazed back. His expression showed that he was pondering the idea. The cards were in his hands. If he wanted, he could kill her right now and discard her body like she was yesterday's trash.

Cartier kept her cool and remained adamant. She refused to have any man see her sweat.

"You talk that shit, but your mouth might bite off more than you can chew. This isn't New York. Down here, I run shit. A snap of my fingers, an' I can have you floating in the Atlantic."

"I know that." Cartier continued her touch against him, and he wasn't stopping it.

Hector glared at her. He really didn't want to just kill her and throw away. Everything about her was stunning, and he yearned for more and more. There was something about Cartier that he just had to have. And even though he was angry with her, he knew she was right — she would be more of an asset to him alive.

"Everybody contributes to the organization."

"And what do you want me to contribute?"

"Loyalty," he responded with a cocksure smile.

Cartier nodded.

He leaned toward her. Now his hand was massaging her thigh. He fixed his eyes on her curvy body in the paisley halter minidress and adjusted himself into the plush leather. "Take off that dress."

There was no fighting it now. Cartier was ready to go all the way with him. This was the inevitable.

She slowly lowered the straps to her dress and sensuously came out of it, her body beaming with perfection. Her eyes were deep and dark and had seen a lot of pain. But her sensual lips were full and made for kissing. Her hips and booty round and succulent, her pussy shaved, she was a beautiful black woman.

Hector wanted to devour her immediately. He leaned in close and kissed her. Her lips tasted like strawberries. His male instincts took over, and his hands started to tour her body, from her tits to her naked hips. He touched her softly. He became intoxicated with her full lips and soft tongue swimming inside his mouth. He cradled the back of her head and marveled at how soft her hair was. Hector's hand roamed freely over her curves. He gently caressed her slim waist and sexy bottom.

Hector began to shed his own clothing. He removed his pants and shoes. Cartier felt for his dick, and surprisingly, she wasn't disappointed by his size. It was nice and hard, eight inches of flesh for her to play with and formidable enough to do the job. Suddenly she was aroused. She could feel the wetness between her legs increase.

Cartier took his flesh into her hands and started to stroke him nicely, causing a stifling groan to be released from his lips. He was leaking pre-come like a teenager. She kissed him again.

"I wanna fuck you now," he growled eagerly in her ear.

Cartier smiled like a schoolgirl. His wish was her command. She straddled his body, her thighs pressed tightly against his sides, his hands full with the curves of her backside. He thrust inside her core, and Cartier jerked, feeling his warm, hard flesh penetrate her like a spear inside of her sensual opening. She felt his dick digging deeper inside of her. Their bodies glued close, every sensation for her was heightened. She grinded her hips into his lap, and they fucked hard in the backseat of the limo as it traveled through downtown Miami.

"Ooooh, fuck me!" she howled. "Ooooh shit! Gotdamn it! So fuckin' good!"

"Ugh! Ugh!" he groaned.

Hector took her nipples into his mouth and sucked hard. He cupped her ass and thrust his throbbing dick upwards into her glorious hole, their bodies moving in harmony, and she enveloped him, providing him with a safe place that felt too good to be true.

Hector scooped her up into his arms like it was nothing, like she belonged to him, and maneuvered Cartier around. He laid her against the plush leather and pressed his body into hers. He pushed himself inside of her. She wrapped her legs around him and closed her eyes. Her breathing became labored, and her chest heaved up and down, betraying her arousal. She was swimming in hormones as Hector pumped his dick inside of her like a piston.

"Fuck me!" she howled as she felt his erection thrusting inside of her vigorously. The intense motion had her lightheaded for a moment. She was about to come. He fucked her harder, pushing her legs against her chest and burying more dick inside of her.

"Oh God! Ooooh shit!"

They went at it for a while, until she exploded like a geyser, her body and legs quivering against him.

It was now his turn, and staring into her beautiful eyes, and being bare against perfection, their heated flesh entwined, he took every delicious inch of her body in, and released inside of her.

They clutched each other and howled. Cartier was spent. She could feel the car still moving. It was some of the best sex she'd ever had.

Hector picked himself up from her sweaty flesh and started to get dressed. Cartier did so also. She took a deep breath and collected herself.

The limo finally came to a stop. They were now fully dressed. Hector stepped out, and Cartier was right behind him, pulling down her minidress, trying to look presentable. She found herself in the middle of nowhere — the marshland, with dirt, grass, and rocks underneath her feet. It looked like the end of civilization, and there was a small house nestled in the cut, something like *Little House on the Prairie*.

She followed him into the godforsaken location. "What is this, Hector?" she asked nervously.

He turned and looked at her, looking smug. "You wanna show me loyalty, right?"

Cartier stood hushed.

"Well, let's see how loyal you truly are." Hector disappeared into the shabby-looking home.

She had nowhere to go. She didn't want to die in the middle of nowhere. Reluctantly, she stepped into the place, and her eyes widened. "Ohmygod! What the fuck is goin' on, Hector?" she shouted.

"This is where your loyalty starts. To keep you alive, and save your life, then you have to take a life," he said coldly.

"But this is ya fuckin' sister!"

"And she's betrayed me one too many times. And I can't have that goin' on in my organization. So she must die."

Quinn was tied with her arms behind her back, slightly beaten, and gagged. She was on her knees. She stared up at Cartier with pleading eyes.

Cartier suddenly had a gun placed in her hand, a 9mm. This was her test, but how could she do it? Quinn had been there for her since day one. She felt twisted and sick.

"You kill her, an' I will go to war for you and keep you under my protection. This right here is where ya loyalty begins with me. This is how you put in work," he said indifferently.

Cartier knew taking Quinn's life would be devastating. She hesitated to pull the trigger.

Hector whispered in her ear, "Think about your family an' your daughter. Think about what those monsters did to her. You owe my sister no favors. But you kill her, an' I promise you, you will get your revenge against the Gonzales Cartel . . . down to the last man."

Tears welled up in Cartier eyes as she locked eyes with Quinn. Quinn began to shake her head violently from hysteria. She wanted Cartier to not give in to her brother's commands. She wanted Cartier to remember everything she had done for her and beg Hector for her life.

Instead Cartier raised the gun to her forehead and took a deep breath. Then she remembered her vow. There was no turning back. She was ready to throw herself into the pits of hell to avenge her daughter, her family, and this was the beginning of hell for her.

Cartier didn't even have the decency to apologize. She pressed the barrel of the 9mm against Quinn's forehead, looking her friend in the eyes. Her tears suddenly stopped, and iciness formed in her eyes.

She squeezed. *Bak!*

Quinn's brains and flesh exploded out the back of her head, and the body dropped quickly at Cartier's feet.

Hector smiled. "That's my girl."

Cartier sighed. Definitely, there was no turning back. She'd shown she was willing to do whatever it took to execute revenge on those who took from her.

❧❦ EPILOGUE ❦❧

Hector had moved Cartier safely to a small bungalow in a beachfront Palm Beach neighborhood. It wasn't exactly a stone's throw from Miami, but it was low-key and safe. A couple weeks had passed since she'd murdered Quinn, and right now she needed to decompress. Hector came to see her at least three nights out of the week. He was making progress with trying to locate the whereabouts of all of the Gonzales Cartel, and he was determined to keep his promise.

The incessant knocking on her front door could only be Hector. It was authoritative and impatient. Hector felt as if he owned Cartier, and she quickly stepped into the shoes of a kept woman. He'd given her the million-dollar bungalow, a midnight-blue Maserati, and shopping sprees to show his appreciation. Hector liked it, so he put a huge diamond ring on it. The eight-karat sparkler caught everyone's attention.

Cartier swung open the front door and her breath hitched. The person standing before her couldn't possibly be real. She blinked a few times before adjusting her focus. The warm smile and confident eyes made her feel nervous.

She could only say one word. "Head."

To be continued...

KEEP READING FOR AN EXCERPT OF
SOUTH BEACH CARTEL
BY NISA SANTIAGO

PROLOGUE

FEBRUARY 1, 2014

I t was a bitter cold day in New York City. The sun was gradually fading behind the horizon and the temperature had dropped to a hazardous ten degrees. The wind nipped at Kola's face like sharp needles as she stood in the Trinity Church Cemetery and Mausoleum. Kola, wrapped in a long, blue Iris mink coat, stood near the graves of three of the most thorough and real women she had ever known. It was hard to believe that they were all dead, including her sister, Apple. Their lives had been violently snatched away from them — they died the way they lived; fast and violent. If Kola had known then what she knew now, she reasoned things would have turned out differently. Your past would always be a part of you—like a shadow. And just because you don't see it all the time doesn't mean it isn't there.

Kola stared at the shiny granite monument as she clutched the small toddler in her arms. The child was maybe the only good thing in her life. She was a beautiful little girl. More precious than a bag of uncut diamonds and equally sought after. The little girl was also wrapped in a beautiful, small mink coat with costly diamonds in her small ears. Even though she was too young to appreciate the quality of clothing and jewelry she had on, Kola had to have the only family in her life looking like wealth.

Her niece was about two years old. Kola didn't know the child's actual birth date, but she thought fondly of future extravagant birthday parties and expensive gifts she'd bestow on the tot. This little girl would be protected by the top security teams and attend the finest private schools. Kola wasn't settling for less.

The adorable child clung to Kola tightly in the frigid cold and was unaware that her mother was dead and was put to rest not too long ago in the scenic plot just a few feet from her. It was a sad moment. Kola looked at the wall of tombs with her twin's name etched into the granite. Even though they'd had their war and feud some time ago, Kola deeply missed her sister. There was a void in Kola's heart where her twin once lived.

"Now what am I supposed to do?" Kola muttered sadly. "I told you not to come back. I told you to stay away."

Apple had refused to listen to Kola's advice. She couldn't accept they had a good thing going on in Columbia.

Kola held the little girl closely and thought about avenging her sister's death. Apple was too young to die, and her death, along with the other two women was so violent. Tears continued to fall from Kola's eyes and her mind was spinning with, *What now? What next? How will the story continue?* Does she give this story—her niece's story a better ending than she and Apple ever had? Kola asked herself, *When does it end?*

Kola looked over her shoulder and saw Eduardo sitting patiently in his chauffeured driven Maybach. The curtains were opened so Eduardo could keep an eye out on the woman he loved.

Parked behind the sleek, black Maybach were two Range Rovers and one Yukon Denali. They were Eduardo's security. Each man was a heavily armed trained killer. They were riding deep considering the circumstances. With power and wealth came jealousy and hate, and Eduardo wasn't taking any chances that a hit could be out on Kola as well.

The cemetery was still. The wind continued to blow hard, but the armed men standing around seemed resistant to the cold. They were clad in dark suits and long black coats. Kola remained motionless, grieving silently. Apple's daughter had been recovered no less than forty-eight hours ago. Apple had given her life for her daughter, and Kola knew the little girl had been through a lot. It was a giant task, but with Eduardo's resources and influence, they found her and brought her back to her family. But the drawback was the girl didn't speak one word of English. She spoke Spanish fluently and was given the name Marisol. Kola knew better. She remembered her sister saying that her baby girl's name was Peaches. Now came the daunting task of communicating with Peaches and helping her adapt to her new surroundings.

Kola took one last look at the graves and inscriptions written across them.

Apple Evans. Gone, but not forgotten.

Cartier Timmons, you will be missed.

Cynthia "Citi" Byrne, a shining star forever.

Kola wondered how three women, as street smart as her sister and her peers, could have been all taken out in one night.

She stepped away from the burial site and walked toward the Maybach. Before she got close, the door was already opened for her by one of the goons. She climbed inside and looked at Eduardo.

"You ready?" Eduardo asked.

Kola nodded.

"Back to Columbia . . . that is your home now, Kola. Forget about this place; forget about the trouble it brings. Your sister will be missed, but you will live on and live on with this precious angel," Eduardo proclaimed.

Kola didn't respond. She closed her eyes and was expressionless. In less than twenty-four hours, she would be back in Colombia. She knew Eduardo was right; there was nothing left for her in the States. This country, America, New York — took away everything.

She opened her eyes narrowly and watched as the headstones of nameless people whisked by her window and hoped that this wouldn't be her fate anytime soon. She wanted to reach her twenty-fifth birthday and knew that the life she was living made the odds a long shot.

Kola felt it was time for a change.

But a voice inside her said, "This is only the beginning."

Follow

MELODRAMA PUBLISHING

www.twitter.com/Team_Melodrama

www.facebook.com/MelodramaPublishing

Order online at
bn.com, amazon.com, and
MelodramaPublishing.com

RISE OF AN AMERICAN GANGSTRESS

RISE OF AN AMERICAN GANGSTRESS

PART 2

Melodrama
PUBLISHING

Kim K.

NATIONAL BESTSELLING AUTHOR OF *SHEISTY CHICKS*

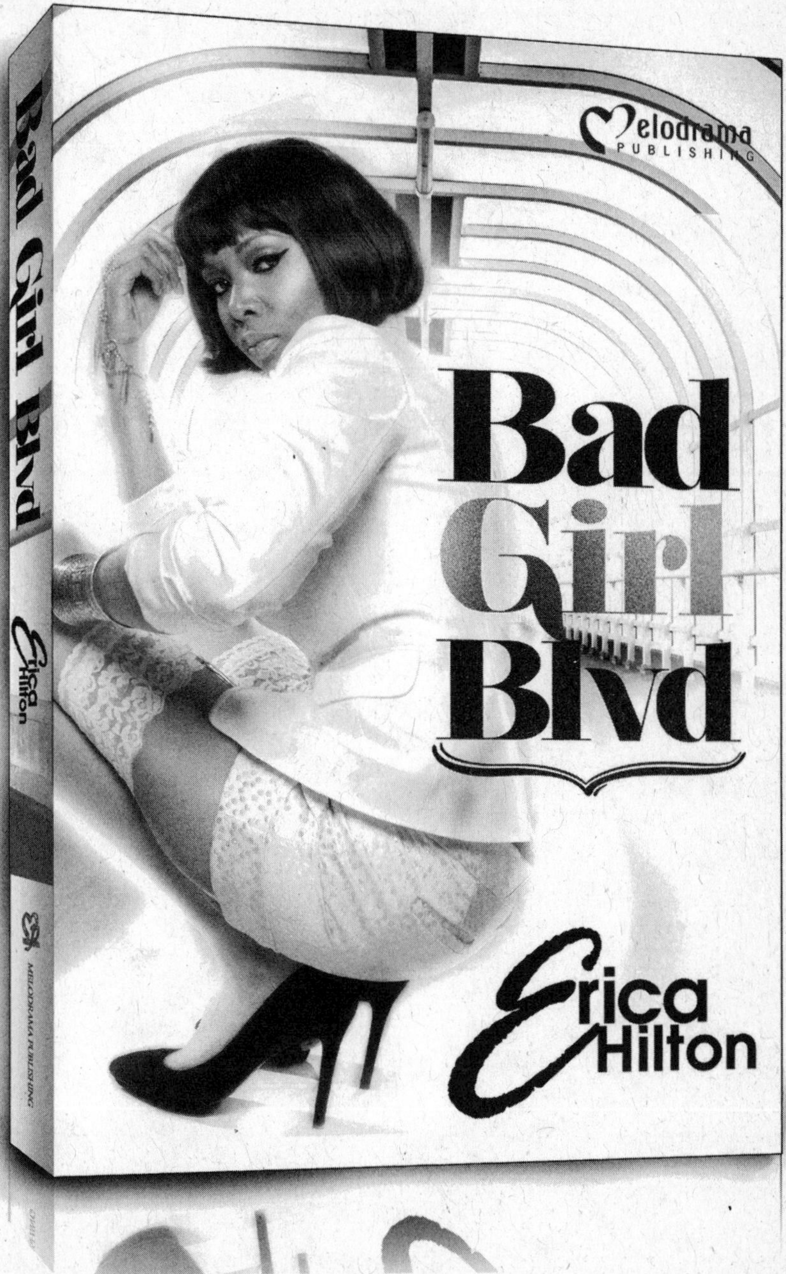
Melodrama
PUBLISHING
Bad
Girl
Blvd
Erica
Hilton
Bad Girl Blvd
Erica
Hilton
MELODRAMA PUBLISHING